SARA GAMARRO

CANTARE ITALIANO
THE LANGUAGE OF OPERA

THE FIRST ITALIAN-BORN METHOD AND COMPLETE GUIDE
TO LYRIC DICTION AND INTERPRETATION OF ITALIAN OPERA

A manual for singers, voice teachers,
vocal coaches, accompanists,
conductors, stage directors, composers

English translation by **Michael Aspinall**

Cover image, "The circle of Italian vowels" © Sara Gamarro
Page 27, image © 123RF/Patrick Guenette
Page 173, photo © Vito Montemurro
Page 175, photo © Adrian Bedford

is a trademark of Volontè & Co. s.r.l.
© 2019 Volontè & Co. s.r.l. - Milano

All rights reserved. No parts of this book may be reprinted or reproduced or utilised in any form or by any electronic, mechanical, or other means, now known or hereafter invented, including photocopying and recording, or in any information storage or retrieval system, without permission in writing from the publishers.

Contents

IMPORTANT NOTE ON THE TRANSLATION	7
Introduction	9

PART ONE - VOICE, VOWELS, VOCAL ART

I. Hints on vocal physiology
Anatomy and transmission	17
Intonation and emission	18
The counterbalance of *the waiter*	20
Features of the voice	22

II. The sung word
Sound and language: *Chinese shadows*	25
Imbalance	28
Vocalizing: not warming up, but therapy	30
Micro-history of vocal music	33

III. Raw material
Seven volumes of light and shade: *chiaroscuro*	41
The circle	44
Fundamental vowel exercise	46
Italian: malleable, but *untouchable*	47
The accents	49
The spaces of the vocalic volumes	52
Let *nothing* have its say	55
Synopsis	57

PART TWO - DICTION, PRACTICE, INTERPRETATION

IV. Rules
How to notate diction	61
Enunciation of vowels	64
Vocalic *crowds*	67
Enunciation of consonants	68
Syntactic germination (or doubling)	70
Balance of the verse and equilibrium of the line	76
Check!	82
Singing Neapolitan	85

V. Errors
Impostures and impostors	87
Chewed legato, *wet* speech	90
When the *letter* becomes threatening	91
What about the *æ?*	93
Arbitrary doubling	94
Syllabication	96

VI. How to study
Step 1: Text	99
Step 2: Psalmody (rhythm + dynamics)	101
Step 3: Melody	102
Learning to *think*: two rules	103
Sight misreading	107

VII. Interpretative diction
The cavatina: learning *to get through it*	109
The Rossini neurosis	111
Cæsar *docet*	117
Nameless buffoons	129
Beats of twin souls	133
Formula for ruling the movement of the stars	136
Whirlwinds of joy	141

Conclusions	**149**
Appendix: Exercises	
How to work	153
The Author	**173**
The Translator	**175**

To my Stella

I would like to acknowledge and thank from the bottom of my heart each and every one of my students, who, throughout seventeen years of teaching singing and eleven of coaching diction and interpretation of Italian Opera, have made me the pioneer I am in this field.

It was for you, out of the desire to reach you and to help you reach your desires, that throughout these years I have theorized, verbalized and exemplified all that I have then been able to write down in this manual.

Thank you for carrying my voice within yours.

I love you all,

la Maestra

IMPORTANT NOTE ON THE TRANSLATION

I support the literary choice of my expert translator, Michael Aspinall, who, in order to preserve as much as possible of my not at all simple original Italian text, opted for using the male pronoun *he* as a generic one, especially whenever I speak of "the singer" – which in Italian is a male noun derived from a verbal form (*il cantante*, present participle of the verb *cantare,* "to sing").

A more gender-neutral, plural pronoun would have in fact made the comprehension of several passages of this book much harder, if not impossible, whereas the choice of a feminine pronoun would have suggested other issues, that are not related to the topic of the book itself.

The choice of *he/his/him/himself* was therefore judged by both of us to be the most neutral, functional and pleasingly literary in the present context.

From now on, the generic pronoun *he* will stand for "the singing human being".

The Author

«Opera has a truly fascinating aspect of madness. What reserves might I have? That I don't know anything about it. Or rather, I do know: **Opera is part of my being Italian**, just like the bersaglieri, Garibaldi, the Roman emperors. Celeste Aida, Questa o quella per me pari sono, Stride la vampa: these voices have accompanied us for ever. I have always had them in my ears. We have seen all our aunts and their daughters weeping over their hand-made lace while they sang Mi chiamano Mimì and our uncles while they roared out passionately Se quel guerrier io fossi.

These things belong to us so much that they become estranged, as is the subconscious.

(....) An insane libretto is set to wonderful music. Then a series of operations takes place that proceed automatically: costumes hired from the costumist, scenery painted somewhere else, lighting placed sporadically here and there... often there is no feeling between conductor and orchestra, singers have given rise to a whole world of anecdotes, they gesture in semaphore and all run to the place onstage from which the voice carries best. And yet, in spite of all these collisions, frictions, impacts, that ought to disintegrate the opera like a centrifugal force, suddenly everything coagulates, **as if it were all drawn together by some eternal law that makes you spin round marvelously.**

(.....) One evening, on TV, I saw an insane transmission of La Traviata. The director (or the cameraman) marched up and down the stage just like an expectant father in a maternity ward, zooming with his lens on everything: on the carpets on the floor, on shoes, on the nails holding the scenery together, on the singers' gold teeth. He was never still a moment. Close-ups that spilled over the screen: so one could understand that the tenor was from Caserta and that the soprano was a Venetian. Well, in spite of the murderous quality of that broadcast, in spite of the singers' faces, in spite of my being alone, with the light on in a little room in my house and every now and then I could hear, from the street below, the wailing sirens of police cars rushing who knows where, in spite of all this, I cried the whole evening long. The first act ended and I was crying. The second act began and, immediately, from the third note, I started to cry again. I was happy to cry. **Perhaps that particular opera, La Traviata, is absolute perfection, a sphere, pure sentiment.** The madman holding the camera had not succeeded in destroying it.

So, if this is the way things are, what can be done that has not already been done by Verdi? To sum up: I don't know, I really don't know anything at all. It is like being called late in the day to decorate an apartment in which the dimensions, the spaces and the colours have already been decided upon. »

Federico Fellini,
Block-Notes di un Regista

Introduction

And today the Italian who asks himself questions, who falls over backwards to discover what constitutes the story of this national reality which makes us feel united, even throughout the immense widening in our differences and despite the conviction that unified Italy is not an absolute value but rather a phase, a transitory historical condition – this Italian who asks himself questions and who wants to identify the nature of his own national consciousness, will discover, God willing, no opaque thickness of flesh and earth, no blind groping of protoplasm and sperm, but rather, everywhere, **the light formed by spirit, the transparency of art, the busy forge of civilization**. *"We have made Italy; now we must make the Italians." When Massimo D'Azeglio pronounced his celebrated phrase he wanted to warn us not to deceive ourselves too much as to the concrete results of a legislative measure that declared the new nation officially constituted, and recognized by the other states of Europe. The new national reality still needed to be built up not only by passing laws, but principally in the consciences of men,*

Massimo Mila,
Verdi

Italian is the *mother tongue* of Opera, since Opera was born in Italy on the foundation of a precise aesthetic project whose fulcrum was, precisely, the language spoken by the inventors of the *genre*. This is explicitly declared by the composer Jacopo Peri in the preface to his *Euridice*, the first opera in history whose complete score has survived, composed by him to the libretto of his friend Ottavio Rinuccini (both of them were members of a *coterie* of artists who met in Florence in the late Renaissance thanks to the munificence of Count Bardi). Peri states that "*the idea was to imitate the spoken word with singing (…..) so that harmony, enhancing that of everyday speech, should arise from melody, from singing, so as to form something between the two.*"

Despite the fact that in theatres throughout all the boot of Italy the people had already for centuries been listening to the common language – Italian – sung by the singers, the poet Ugo Foscolo, at the time of the Unification of Italy, could write that "*…a man from Bologna and a man from Milan cannot understand each other, except by making an enormous effort*". And yet, in the Opera house Italy had already been unified, thanks to the language, and the State of Opera would continue to exist until our times – from 1600 until after the invention of YouTube – moreover, expanding exponentially first with the invention of the gramophone record and then through internet.

Despite all this, curiously, no manual of Italian operatic diction written by an Italian author and published by an Italian publisher has been issued until now: it seems incredible; this prevents us Italians from complaining about any slovenliness, at home or abroad, that might have been perpetrated so far to the detriment of Italy's most precious and *constituent* national patrimony. This text-book of mine is arriving more than one hundred and fifty years late with respect to Garibaldi's unification and more than twenty with respect to the unification of Europe, which has poured a flood of Erasmus students (added to those hailing from Asia, even greater in number, plus all the others) into Italian universities and conservatories. It comes to fill one of those gaps typical of new organizations – such as Italy is – after having practically written itself during the past ten years of my specialized teaching practice in the subject; and it comes, at the historic moment in which the Italian language is already yielding place to English (which is taking over the role that once belonged to Latin), aiming precisely at repeating that, even when Italy might hypothetically be once more losing her national geographic borders, the State of Opera, on the other hand, stretching along the boot of Italy from Donizetti's Bergamo to Bellini's Catania – can never be lost, and so it is with its language, which is the *matrix* and the *basic material* of the *genre*.

Italian singing, therefore, cannot be reduced to a merely orthoepical matter: we are dealing with an *ontologically musical* affair: singing *is* Italian, Italian *is* singing. There cannot be any vocal technique without a knowledgeable *vowel formation technique* of the Italian language. This implies that the singer's diction must be understood as consisting only in part as merely facilitating the understanding by the audience of the words being sung: the higher this level of intelligibility is, the better it is – it goes without saying – but, significantly, correctness of diction in singing has a great effect, perhaps an even greater effect, on an audience that does not understand the language being sung, as they do not speak it: as if the correct diction contained a magical component of *enchantment*[1] upon audiences, almost

---

[1] «The dead are beings who sing though petrified. The Spanish language has preserved this ideal megalithic connection between *canto* and *pietra* ("singing" and "stone") in the word *canto*. *Encantar* must originally have meant not only "to cast a spell", but also "turn to stone by singing".»; Marius Schneider, *Il significato della Musica*, Rusconi, 1979. In Italian as well *canto* ("the act of singing"), *cantiere* ("construction yard") and *canto* ("angle, corner stone") share the same etymon.

apart from the content being transmitted. The *poetic* word is, in fact, by definition *creative: poetry* comes from the Greek *poièo*, meaning "*I make, I create, I model*". If a word does not produce a concrete and *meta-linguistic* reality, it has been badly pronounced and robbed of its *poetry*. Furthermore, most of the great arias in Opera are great soliloquies, which the character sings without being heard by anyone beside himself (if every singer kept this fact in mind, many more indications of *pp*, *ppp* and *pppp* would be respected). The singer's duty, therefore, rather than making the words clear, should be to create for himself an *interior voice* of the character, giving utterance, though through the medium of words, to his *meta-verbal* soul, using what in this manual we will generally refer to as *interpretative diction*.

This manual does not exist, therefore, to tell the reader if a vowel is open or closed, except occasionally and only with the intention of pointing out to him some other more structural concept; this is *not* what we mean, here, by *diction!* Furthermore, this kind of everyday information is available today at a mere click[2] and, whenever needed, more rapidly put to use than by reading this book. The object of this little treatise will, if anything, be the emotion that opens or closes a vowel, or that a vowel means to disclose to the human soul according to the musical and dramaturgical intentions of the composer in demanding *that* particular word from the librettist in *that* particular position; it will be the history behind a lemma; sometimes it will be free associations on its root word; it will be the genetic content of its *DNA*; and much more besides.

The great English stage director Peter Brook, in an interview[3], compared Opera as it is understood by today's market to a crumbling building whose pipes, which once carried water, had progressively rusted and deteriorated to the point in which people had forgotten their original function, transforming the building itself into a museum whose very *walls* (i.e. the essential matter) were torn down with the incomprehensible aim of admiring the empty tubes in ecstasy.[4] The aim of this text is to praise the ancient

---

[2] The reader is recommended to consult the *Treccani* dictionary, available online and always reporting the etymon and the orthoepy – the correct diction – of words.

[3] Discussion with Charlie Rose, 2003.

[4] Peter Brook, *Op. Cit.*: "You come to Mozart and find a perfect marriage between the artificial and something that is fully alive – here's an example: the rigid pipe and the water flowing through it. But

beauty and the functionality of those tubes, but in the hope that pure water may once more run through them and that this water may bring back a thirst for so long unjustly frustrated that it has dried up in audiences.

Riccardo Muti has recently[5] and perhaps rather provocatively claimed that no opera staging can be better than the one that each member of the audience has in his own mind, when his imagination is stimulated exclusively by the *audible instruments* of music and words. One might agree or not, but, in fact, when we listen to an opera over the radio or on a recording, we have no choice but this: to create for ourselves a vision starting from the poetic sound. Furthermore, we know very well how far historical memory and the cult of the art form even today lean upon certain legendary disc recordings of the past (of most of which no corresponding video material exists): just *listening* to them, they have forged our taste and nurtured our *visual imagery* for decades. It is therefore essential that students make a profound and accurate study of the libretto, making the text so malleable as to furnish the singer and the listener with the necessary instruments for creating their *own* production of the opera: this preliminary study, necessary and sometimes enough to guarantee the success of a production, may be considered one of the few new frontiers possible to the *avant-garde* of stage production, given the rigid structure of Opera's market. When such a study of *interpretative diction* exists and when it is well constructed, it will cast the *spell* and work the magic; never mind the rest – whatever that may be[6].

---

gradually the attention begins to go more and more to the artificial until suddenly you're into sclerosis. Suddenly that pipe is taking all the attention and less and less water is trickling through it. Finally you get a fundamentally unwell and crazy society in which people forget that pipes were put into buildings for the purpose of letting the water through, and they now consider them to be works of art. People knock the walls down and admire the piping and totally forget its original purpose and function. This is what happened in many art forms, and Opera is the clearest example."

[5] In an interview on the occasion of the opening ceremonies of the XXVIII edition of the Ravenna Festival, 2017.

[6] The quotation by Federico Fellini that we opened this book with is taken from his *Block-notes di un regista* ("A director's notebook"), published by Longanesi in 1988. A whole chapter of the book is dedicated to Opera, and it was written by Fellini with the sole purpose of explaining the reasons why he never, ever agreed to direct an operatic production, in spite of the incredibly generous offers made to him at the time by the administrators of the most important Opera houses in the world (the then administrator of the Metropolitan Opera House, New York offered the director a whole trip across the United States in order to convince him: Fellini accepted the trip, but eventually turned down the commission).

PART ONE
VOICE, VOWELS, VOCAL ART

I. Hints on vocal physiology

When you speak, the sound flows from your mouth like a wave
overflowing from an over-filled basin.
It impregnates your body and spreads through it.
Every syllabic wave flows over you and spreads through you,
Without your realizing it, but surely.

Alfred Tomatis,
The Ear and the Voice

The physiology of the act of phonation consists of an extremely complicated apparatus, involving more than a hundred muscles in a singer's body: it is therefore useless to try to acquire physical and mechanical control of it. However, here we shall try to briefly describe it, greatly simplifying it and illustrating the little that it seems to us useful to know about it, not so much with the intention of doing anything special once we know about it, but rather to avoid inadvertently doing useless things: in the art of singing, economy means concentration; and concentration, success.

Anatomy and transmission

The voice diffuses its vibrations within the singer's body, not through the air, but through the *solid* path, passing through the skeleton; for this reason Alfred Tomatis[7] defines the good singer's voice as *osseous voice*. The reactor emitting these vibrations is also a part of the bone structure and is called the *larynx*: it is a hollow cartilage, placed at the front middle of the throat. It is almost always visible in the adult male, in whom it is significantly known as the *Adam's apple*: this indicates the divine and ancestral heritage of the human voice, besides confirming that the *word* – the *logos*, that opens John's Gospel[8] and traces of which we find in any other early culture – is the origin

---

[7] Alfred Tomatis, *The Ear and the Voice*, Scarecrow Press, 1987.

[8] «In the beginning was the Word, and the Word was with God, and the Word was God.» - John 1:1.

and beginning of all things (just as Adam is the "putative father" of humanity[9]).

When we sing in the *listening posture*[10] (continuing to use the terminology crystallized by the studies of the inspired French otorhinolaryngologist, whose books we urge singers to consult without reserve) the larynx enters into contact with the first vertebra and in this way favours transmission through the bones, i.e. *dry transmission* of vocal vibrations, which will travel into the *resonance cavities* of the cranium to resound and make themselves audible.

The larynx is internally lined with a mucous membrane forming two pairs of symmetrical folds, placed vertically at a short distance one above the other and named the *vocal cords* and the *false vocal cords*: here we shall deal with only the former and the sounds they produce. The *vocal cords* are joined at the anterior portion and flow together into the *thyroid*, upon whose hormones largely depends their growth in length and thickness, and therefore the type of sound that they will emit (a reason why the *Adam's apple* is visible from the exterior mostly in men: a bigger larynx will have correspondingly long and thick cords, giving a lower sound and a darker timbre).

Intonation and emission

In order to reproduce the note imagined by the singer (quite apart from whether or not the note is then emitted), his vocal cords stretch as the effect of a mere *impulse of the brain* which puts in motion a complex system of little arytenoid cartilages. These make the cords converge at a certain point of their length, reducing the posterior portion which remains free long enough to produce the note at the desired pitch. This shortening, or *adduction*, will affect a different portion of the cords according to the *height* of the note (although you should be careful not to envision a sound as *high* or *low,* in order to avoid false visual and spatial associations, potentially

---

[9] «The Brahmanic myths of creation relate that the first men were transparent beings, luminous and sonorous, who flew above the earth. Only once they came down to earth and began to eat plants did they lose their lightness and their peculiar luminosity. Their bodies became opaque and the only thing left of their musical substance was their voice.»; Marius Schneider, *Singende Steine*.

[10] Alfred Tomatis, *op.cit.*

dangerous to the act of phonation; the Italian language comes in help, here, for it calls the high notes *acuti*, which simply means "narrow, piercing"). The mechanism of correctly tuning the voice is therefore similar to that of any other string or bowed instrument, but with the important difference that, while on an instrument the shortening of the cord would be effected manually, in the case of the singer the adduction of the cords is – we repeat – an *unconscious* phenomenon: in other words, you only need to think the note in your own mind and it will instantly be sounded, apart from the fact that the sound will effectively then be emitted, as has been amply observed and documented.

In order for the sound to become more audible, the cords must, besides adducing, also be set in *vibration*. This mechanical motion pertains to the *breath*, which, however, must always intervene in minimum quantities and be carefully managed, whatever the dynamics of the music might require (essayists of Belcanto talk about *mastering one's own breath*[11]), in order to avoid such phenomena as dyspnea, tiredness, hyperventilation or even the cracking of the note, if a brusque jet of air coming from the *trachea* separates the cords during the act of adduction.[12]

The function and the flow of breath in singing ends here: the pseudo theories and techniques according to which the air gets "directed" into some area or other of the cranium – in other words, the resonators – are to be dismissed as pure illusion: the propagation of sound vibration that concerns the singer's *self-listening* and control of his instrument takes place exclusively by the *solid* path.

---

[11] Manuel Garcia Jr., *Traité complet de l'art du chant*.

[12] We take this opportunity to stress the fact that the frequent little gusts of air voluntarily inserted by singers between the notes in rapid passages of agility in a certain repertory (such as the Rossinian) constitute a bad habit, founded on lack of skill in *vowel treatment* as well as on doubtful aesthetic taste, which is very harmful to the health of the cords (as would be, for a player on the electric bass guitar, the exclusive use of *slapping*, the technique of smacking the strings; eventually blisters and then *corns* would form on the bass player's fingertips: nothing too alarming here, for corns would be helpful; instead, when *nodules* form on the singer's vocal cords, the surgeon must be called in).

The counterbalance of *the waiter*

The "vis insita", or innate force of matter, is a power of resisting, by which every body, as much as in it lies, endeavours to persevere in its present stale – whether it be of rest, or of moving uniformly forward in a right line.
This force is ever proportional to the body whose force it is; and differs nothing from the inactivity of the mass, but in our manner of conceiving it.
A body, from the inactivity of matter, is not without difficulty put out of its state of rest or motion. Upon which account, this "vis insita", may, by a most significant name, be called "vis inertia", or force of inactivity.
But a body exerts this force only when another force, impressed upon it, endeavours to change its condition; and the exercise of this force may considered both as resistance and impulse;
it is resistance, insofar as the body, for maintaining its present state, withstands the force impressed;
it is impulse, in so far as the body, by not easily giving way to the impressed force of another, endeavours to change the state of that other.
Resistance is usually ascribed to bodies at rest, and impulse to those in motion; but motion and rest, as commonly conceived, are only relatively distinguished; nor are those bodies always truly at rest, which commonly are taken to be so.

Isaac Newton,
Philosopiæ Naturalis Principia Mathematica

In order for the flow of breath that caresses the cords to remain constant and regular for the whole length of the phrase, the singer needs a precise technique for regulating the use of the *breath* – but this as long as the *listening posture* be always maintained, the best possible transmission of the vibrations to the resonators is guaranteed and as long as the throat (*gola*, or *gorgia*, from which we get *gorgheggio*: "a florid vocal exercise") is always left relaxed and free of tensions (usually tension is caused by a faulty conception of the *diction* of the words or by an incorrect search for intonation by mechanical means).

A *technique for regulating the use of the breath*, not a "breathing technique", it must be stressed, because breathing in itself remains a natural, unconscious act, as it is in our first moment of life. The aim is to have, and to maintain in the art of singing, its first, original vital function, both regenerating and restorative. We must therefore keep in mind that the act of *inhaling and exhaling air* is not necessarily the same thing as *breathing*: breathing is the thing that we do automatically, instinctively, because we need to, without realizing that we are doing it; which must remain true also when we are singing and we have the possibility of foreseeing and planning when to take breaths.

This technique of controlling the breath, which merely restricts the innate respiratory gesture, has been fixed by Belcanto in the two concepts of *appoggio* and *sostegno*, which are complementary and for this reason described in terms that are not synonymous, as is often erroneously thought, but rather define contrary movements in synergy, which, in an expert singer, come into action simultaneously and reciprocally, at the same time that he mentally imagines the sound, shaping it from the very breathing.

This synergy, involving a vast system of muscles and which we can feel mostly in the *intercostal* and *dorsal* regions, aims at creating in the singing body a *counter-weight* to the sound being sung, endowing the singer extemporarily with the most suitable *resonance chamber* for containing and rendering audible what he has imagined. This *counter-weight* must always limit itself to being just that. In other words, it must be necessary and sufficient for the sound desired: it must never be less than the amount necessary, to avoid the sound being *unsupported*, nor must it be excessive, to avoid its being *pushed* (sometimes these two extremes may get mixed up or coincide).

The *appoggio* and the *sostegno* may be happily represented by the picture of a *waiter* who has to carry alternately on his tray or in his hand dishes of different weight; at this point he will automatically counterbalance the weight of a cup of coffee (the *appoggio*) with a corresponding support (*sostegno*) from his arm (and his whole body) enough to prevent him from dropping it, but not strong enough to send it flying away; if he has to carry a full stewpot to the table, the support offered by our waiter will be of quite another quantity, but his objective will always stay the same: that of never overturning or slopping anything, to maintain the physical *status quo* and to serve liquid and boiling hot first courses with the same *nonchalance* with which he will later carry the bill.

The skill of the singer also consists in giving the perfect *counter-weight* to any *weight* of sound, so that, like the waiter's tray, his working surface constantly remains stable, and his vocal line suffers no dangerous ripples or cracks.

Thanks to the technique of restraint and dosage of the *appoggio* and the *sostegno*, the rib cage and all the sounding-board are able to remain loosely expanded and reactive for the whole duration of the musical phrase, in this way maintaining the *diaphragm* muscle deliberately flat, almost independently of the effective quantity of air remaining in the lungs. It must always be remembered that this muscle, the cornerstone of whole theories and vocal methods, acts *involuntarily* and is for this reason irrelevant to the practical aims of the singer: its function is purely to separate the *apparatuses* dealing with inspiration and digestion, from which its name comes (from the Greek, *dià-phragma*: "that which interposes itself", "that lies between"), since the lungs are two sponges under constant pressure, automatically sucking in and expelling air to guarantee the body its regular supply of oxygen and the expulsion of carbon dioxide.

The singer should consciously try only to generate a temporary and voluntary *restraint* of this air so that it is useful for singing, indirectly maintaining the vocal work surface (as well as the *diaphragm/tray*) nicely level and stretched thanks to the posture, which in this way will match the ideal *listening posture* (recommended by Tomatis and mentioned above), and all the muscular system involved with it.

Waiters, it is true, have an impeccable posture: not only for aesthetic reasons of elegance, but also for a physical necessity of constantly having to unload the weights they are carrying onto a support; who knows, perhaps they sing well, too.

Features of the voice

Once more making use of our former metaphor we will say that, just as not all heavy weights – or light ones – can easily be supported by all waiters, it goes without saying that not all types of repertory can be supported by all singers, either for excess or for lack of either vocal weight or of physical counter-weight.

The *timbre*, the *range* and the *tessitura* (that is, the register most frequented) of the singer's voice depend most certainly on physical features – one of them being the sex at birth, which through hormones determines the structure and dimensions of the vocal cords, larynx and all the resonators. (For this reason, throughout the XVII and XVIII centuries, the cruel practice of castration of vocally gifted boys before puberty was established, in order to preserve the colour and extension of their soprano or alto voices, but in the bigger and more resonant male bodies, so to make vocal monsters of them.) Other factors include *hearing* and *language*: factors that today are plausibly reputed to be the cause, and not the consequence, of some of these physical features and that are determinative in rendering each voice absolutely unique, and yet in some way creating similarities between those voices coming from the same geographical area (we talk of typical "Italian voices", as we do of "Korean sopranos", "Russian basses", "Argentinian tenors", etc.).

Such a system of interconnections generating and constantly filling out the singer's voice, and being itself informed by the voice, determining all its possible characteristics and qualities, is happily termed *audio-vocal circuit* by Tomatis.[13]

> To recapitulate: we should breathe as we do when talking and not thinking about it, according to how much we want to say and how we mean to say it, while a cerebral impulse will bring the cords together; and here is where the breath intervenes: dosed – that is, released in a controlled manner, thanks to the synergy of the appoggio and sostegno – and makes the cords vibrate. This vibration involves the whole larynx; the larynx passes the vibrations on by solid contact with the first vertebra and to all the resonating bones. This is what happens in the case of all expert singers.

In singing, this mechanism of phonation goes in parallel with *language, simple utterance*.[14]

---

[13] Alfred Tomatis, *Op. Cit.*

[14] «In Belcanto the school of breathing is the school of the muscles governing breathing and phonation»; Antonio Juvarra in *Mozart 2006* of 21 September 2015.

II. The sung word

Let not thy left hand know what thy right hand doeth.

Matthew, 6:3

Sound and language: *Chinese shadows*

People take it for granted that language is sonorous, but this is not so: the articulation of *phonemes* in the languages that we speak and hear spoken, just like the concatenation of *graphemes* when we write and read them, is nothing but a *code*, completely abstract. And though language comes to life – from the beginning – from the universe of sound with the aim of synthesizing it[15], it only acquires its independence after a while, but then maintains it: think of the internal dialogue that we all have, that goes everywhere with us (in our thoughts, in our reading), produced and understood even by those who for whatever reason have lost their use of speech or hearing; or think of the so-called *dead languages* or of any unknown linguistic code that our eyes light upon, which, although we recognize it as such, does not awaken in our minds any sound or meaning whatsoever.

This abstract and mute language comes together with the vocal sound in the synergic production of the *word*, whether this is *spoken* or *sung* (let it not be forgotten that, from the physiological point of view, *speaking* and *singing* are qualitatively the same thing, the difference being only a matter of quantity, varying the intensity and the duration of sounds). During this collaboration, however, *language* and *sound*, although developing and nurturing each other, remain for ever separated in their production and management, which, in fact, happen to be the prerogative of different *hemispheres of the brain*: language is understood and produced by the *left brain*, whereas sound is processed by the *right brain*. The two brains do not

---

[15] Not always: see the case of invented languages, like *Esperanto* or like the languages elaborated by Tolkien in *The Lord of the Rings*; all in their origin detached from sound reality and yet endowed with their own inherent coherence that makes them intelligible and speakable, even though they are not actually practical, for they don't come from a geographical sound reality (see note 24), and so are not long-living.

appear to have any physical interconnection between each other, even though they interact constantly: only in the case of cerebral pathology, such as *ictus* or hemorrhage, can we observe the effects of the disassociation of these two co-operators – effects that vary according to whether it is the left or the right side that is involved in the pathology.[16]

Although always remaining physically separate from its source, therefore, language models and permeates sound, and, doing this, contributes to the projection of a third reality, which is the *word* (in our case, the sung word).

To present this <u>idea</u> in an image, we might say that language is to sound as the hands are to the light in the art of *Chinese shadows*. We all know the game of Chinese shadows and will have tried at least once to reproduce figures with the hands in front of a ray of light (without putting the hands directly *on* the light source, one hopes: let us keep this wise precaution in mind, because it is valid in singing, too), entertaining ourselves by seeing a living creature projected onto the surface upon which the light was directed. And all of us have marveled when this projection acquired its completed form on the wall: a form that could not be seen if we looked directly at our hands; and yet, that convoluted web of fingers was able to project dogs, elephants and rabbits onto the wall. *Mutatis mutandis*, all of this also takes place in the act of singing, when we pronounce sung words in perfect sense in a certain language. The sung word, with its dynamic and ductile capacities, is the equivalent of the projected shadow, in the game of Chinese shadows.

The projected shadow is therefore a *third, separate entity*, that takes on life from the movement of the hands produced simultaneously with the ray of light (identically, the sung word is a third, separate entity that takes on life from the mental articulation of language produced simultaneously with the undulating vocal flow). Such a shadow could not exist in the absence of even just one of its two generating components, but it *always* remains distinct and separated from both.

---

[16] Jill Bolte Taylor, *My Stroke of Insight*, Penguin Books, 2006.

The projection becomes an independent, third entity[17] to the extent that, once sketched out on the wall (which is the singer's self-listening), it is always to that projection that we turn to get our bearings when modifying our work: while adjusting it we look at the wall, not at our hands themselves, which meanwhile continue to fumble until the visible image is exactly what we wanted.

At this point – and this is just as true for the singer learning to vocalize as it is for the child learning to speak – it will be the accuracy of the result, that is, its correspondence with the idea that evoked it, together with the satisfaction it arouses, that will create in us – eventually, by constant repetition – also the *physical memory* of the movement and of the position necessary to sustain the excellence of that shape through time. In other words, we must develop a muscular automatism as a consequence of the search for the *correct vowels;* but to this end it is clear that we must first know how to envision those vowels in our mind. This practice will help the singer, furthermore, to acquire ever greater rapidity and precision as time goes by, never forgetting, however, the inevitable margins of adaptation due from time to time to variables such as the singer's psycho-physical condition, or the environmental and acoustical conditions of the performance[18].

---

[17] To get a clearer idea of the separation of sound and language, and keeping to our metaphor of Chinese shadows, let us say: can a light be lit without hands necessarily moving in front of it? Certainly: sound can exist without being classed by a particular language. Can hands move in the dark, where there is no light? Yes to this too: there can be language without sound (see note 15). Can any kind of surface potentially suitable for the projection of *Chinese shadows* exist even in the absence of a light source, or of a child who wants to try to project the shadow of a dog onto it? Yes: the case of a *listener* in the *silence* could arise. In our case the projection or receiving surface is *hearing* – in primis the singer's hearing of his own voice, or what Tomatis calls *self-listening*. Just as the exceptional case might arise of a rabbit so well constructed and so well articulated in its movements as to take on truly lifelike movements in our eyes, going so far as to make us forget that it is only the fruit of *illusionism* (an *acoustic illusion* in this case of ours): and that is the case of an expert singer, when singing.

[18] Laura Habegger, *Apprendimenti motori e pratica strumentale*, essay published in the Italian magazine *Musica Domani* in 2005.

Even an automatism, even a *good* automatism, is never absolute, nor definitive: the finest literary example of this fact is once again to be found in Tomatis[19], who describes his meeting with the great Italian tenor Beniamino Gigli, and what had become his regular study practice, once he had reached a certain age:

"Although I was very excited by what Gigli was saying, I did not understand what he was talking about. However, after I told him about my experiments with audio-vocal reactions and how the ear modifies the voice, he responded by telling me in detail how he had recovered 'his' vowels. Having chosen what he considered to be his best recordings, he listened to them with headphones while looking in a mirror. He reshaped his vowels by listening. The recordings he used were 'Cielo e Mar' from La Gioconda and 'M'apparì' from Marta. He said: "By training in this way, I realized that I had started to open my sounds too much; I was off the track. After realizing that, I was happy just to make the vowel shapes in front of a mirror without singing. I exercised by simulating each aria in this way, in vocal silence, strictly observing the shape and size of the vowel".

Belcanto is, therefore, co-existence and synergy, but with absolute independence, of two parallel worlds, of two separate hemispheres: sound and language. Now that we know this, let us never forget it.

Imbalance

What happens in this synergetic balance which is singing, when one of the two component generators begins to dominate over the other and the balance creating the perfect illusion is broken? It happens that certain defects become evident, rather typical and diffused among singers, but sometimes also typical of certain vocal styles, especially if they are outside the world of what we call classical music.

One is the *voce intubata* ("hooty voice"), typical of the singer who neglects the verbal component and gives priority to a certain hoped – for quality of the voice, which is usually the so-called *roundness;* by doing this, however, the singer, will progressively lose brilliance and ring, acquiring an ever wider and more unnatural vibrato, which, in a vicious circle, will come to completely

---

[19] *Op. Cit.*

ruin hearing and even physical balance (the ear being responsible not only for hearing but also for equilibrium and *posture*).

The opposite of the *hooty voice* is the *voce ingolata* ("throaty voice"), typical of those who, very badly interpreting the Monteverdian concept of *recitar cantando*[20], deform the discourse by subduing it to the *intonation*: the throaty singer chokes or chips his own discourse in the search for the desired note (not knowing that he would have it "right there" if he only knew how to take it – and we use the locution *to take a note* precisely because we are dealing with *receiving* something, not with a production of our own; with *a syntonization with an already existing vibration*, which is seized by our ear and reflected through our bodies). The throaty singer deforms his own discourse, compromising its isolation, its abstract quality and its ideal Belcanto independence.

The fact that we can talk and be understood even while we are asleep (the phenomenon of *somniloquism*, or talking in your sleep), or the fact that there are people who know how to make themselves understood without moving a muscle (the phenomenon of *ventriloquism*), should give us an idea of to what extent muscles are superfluous to the production of comprehensible sung words.

One might also mention the *voce coperta* ("covered voice"[21]: with this expression we mean that the vowel and therefore the *word* is covered, or *veiled* from the sight of the audience, skillfully produced without disturbing either the emission of the voice or the facial features) and, as its opposite, the *voce scoperta* ("uncovered voice": when the singer emits sound and word as if they were one and the same thing, once again deforming the discourse by subjugating it to the intonation, visibly shifting and deforming the vocal apparatus). Again from *The Ear and the Voice*:

---

[20] *Recitar cantando* was the name given to the new style of singing according to which the first operas were written, at the dawn of the XVII century.

[21] Let us take the opportunity to clarify that here *covering* is by no means used to mean the application to the sound of those fashionable cheek and palate gimmicks that are eagerly embraced by singing teachers, quite the reverse: with this expression we simply mean that *the word* is well *concealed* – both visually and acoustically, its phonemes being thus skillfully "melted" in a soft flow of sound and therefore of muscle – its mental diction remaining though crystal clear, to guarantee the ring, the health, literally the "good shape" of every sound.

«*Gigli was right. Singing is essentially a business of making vowels. You must know how to focus them so they do not become a problem in singing. in such a manner that they do not interfere with the singing. It comes down to the fact that there is one part of the body subject to the musician, the composer, a part that he himself would have sung if he had been capable of it, and another part belonging to the author of the words who, in no case, would have been able to interfere with the preceding phenomenon. Everything was suddenly all made clear to me or, at least, it seemed to get clearer. Now I had to discover the place where vowels are formed, how they are formed and developed. In truth it was not so simple, but I knew that I was on the right path. It seemed obvious to me that these volumes, belonging to vowels, must be found in the mouth. Certainly, it still had to be determined how it could be possible to realize the cavities in such a way that they would not interfere with the generating sound, in this case the "laryngeal reactor."*»

This is a very nice definition of the concept of *covering*, so abused elsewhere, as reported in the description of the great tenor Gigli: *covering*, therefore, far from being an artificial mechanism, is the quintessence of *inaction;* it is the complete relaxation in muscular tension of the throat, making singing independent of it, it is the typical attitude of profound emotions like sobbing, orgasmic joy, sexual excitement (that is, the essential themes dealt with by Opera libretti).

A story apart is the *voce affondata*, based on what is supposed to be a technique of emission called *dell'affondo* ("of lowering of the larynx") by those practicing it: we shall not take up any time discussing this, to avoid publicizing a concept that, apart from being mistaken and unhistorical, is completely false and fictional.

Vocalizing: not warming up, but therapy

The daily practice with which the singer is inoculated to pursue the goal of acquiring vocal automatism is the *vocalise*: there exist whole books of them, of every description and datable to more or less every period of Music history, but let whoever sings mainly the Belcanto repertoire (and whoever, banally, happens to be Italian) remember that to sing, to speak, to listen and first of all and above all to know how to *imagine* a sung Italian that is educated and correct is already, to every effect, *vocalization*. For the foreign singer it will be absolutely *indispensable* to focus properly the vowel *volumes* of Italian, with the help of a good teacher (who should be a native Italian speaker or who should have equal mastery of the language[22]: an exceptional yet not impossible occurrence), but even our native singers are not exempt from such thorough research (Gigli *docet*) and to vocalize on fifths, ninths or thirteenths on the unadorned Italian vowels might certainly be a way to study and to gain mastery over these archetypical forms, but certainly it is not the only way and not necessarily the most efficient.

The entire body of *arie antiche italiane*[23], for example, gets the same results, at the same time ensuring that aspects such as *musicianship* and *dynamics* are not neglected; just as the greater number of the *cavatine* in operatic rôles were conceived *ad hoc* by the composer, working together with the librettist, with the idea of offering the singer, embedded in text and the piece, the *vocalises* needed to warm the voice up in the right way and on the vowels useful for taking on the rest of the rôle; of *that* rôle. In fact, not all the selections and characters, even not all the situations that the same character finds himself in, require from the singer the same voice and the same manner of delivering the text, so the practice of using *vocalises* cannot be one and the same (as often happens after years of stale practicing) for preparing yourself to sing *anything* at all: warming up must be adapted to whatever you have to then *actually* sing, otherwise it is useless, if not damaging and misleading; and tiring!

> *Reminder*: since the brain is the home of the vowels (*vocali*), it is consequently the home of the *vocalise* as well.

It will therefore be more useful, to the end of properly preparing *all the body* for the vocal act, to begin from the *brain*, ensuring it the right quantity and quality of *food* and *sleep*, and then "waking it up" with a light *physical* warm-

---

[22] That is "who has mastered its *prosody* and *sounds*" – let it be understood – apart from whether one might speak it or not; in 90% of cases, unfortunately, foreign languages become influenced by the bandwidth of one's own mother tongue and so distorted, even where the languages have been perfectly mastered on the lexical and grammatical level.

[23] We recommend the collection edited by Dall'Albero and Candela and entitled *Celebri arie antiche. Le più note arie del primo barocco italiano trascritte e realizzate secondo lo stile dell'epoca*, published by this same Rugginenti Editore in 1988.

up (yoga, stretching, dance, walking, housework: each to his own), from which the brain above all will benefit, together with its capacity for concentration, thanks to the increase in oxygen. To clean the vocal cords it is enough to clear the voice with the classic "*a-hem*" and then it is enough to begin speaking or singing (as we have already seen, it is enough just to *think* of doing this, and the cords will already do their duty): we cannot "warm up the voice", for the voice in itself does not exist, as it is the resultant of many concurring factors.

All this, naturally, is true *in general*, or rather for the singer who only needs to warm up before beginning the musical work on and with his voice.

The case will be different with a singer, at whatever point in his study or career, who is undertaking an adjustment or even a correction of certain aspects of his singing and for whom one or more *vocalises* are administered by the teacher, but *wisely*, always just for a certain period, limited in duration – as a specific *therapy* and specially designed for the problems to be dealt with. We welcome a *staccato* on the vowel *u* as a remedy for a voice too *white* or choked in pronunciation, or long scales on the vowel *i* to eliminate an overdone vibrato and problems of adduction of the cords, but these will always be temporary and the good teacher will take care to change them from lesson to lesson, so as to stimulate the pupil to seek out new roads, to make him explore new solutions without making him fall back on his old habits, from which he should be encouraged to abstain. It is significant, and should be cause for reflection, that many "problematic" singers start to sing better when, often through exasperation, they stop singing or going to lessons for long periods. *Vocalises* and specific exercises may well be useful, for example, for those with nodules on the vocal cords, or even those who have recently undergone an operation on them, but this is not the place for examining such extreme cases. The rule is and remains this: a *vocalise* may be a valid medicine if it is used on special occasions, but becomes dangerous if it is used daily without a specific reason; the *vocalise* therefore does not serve to *warm up* the voice on a daily basis, especially if it is always the same one for months or years, the danger being the confirming of stale mental and *muscular* habits of no help to *musical* or vocal action, which as a result will gradually become less and less inspired, genuine, artistic.

You must never allow the pupil to detach himself emotionally from his own vowels and his own vocalizing, turning it into a habitual practice of *stretching*.

Whenever there is a need to vocalize, let it be done at a different time of day from the time in which *singing* and *interpreting* are practiced. Very often – alas – getting used to singing a certain *vocalise* serves only to learn to sing *that vocalise* (*if* that). How much better to warm up by singing the piece itself to be sung, following steps that will be illustrated in more detail in the second part of this treatise, which will concentrate more specifically on the practice of diction.

Micro-history of vocal music

> *[....] et udi' sospirando dir parole che farian gire I monti et stare I fiumi [....]*
> And I heard whispered words that would spin mountains and halt rivers
>
> Francesco Petrarca,
> Canzoniere

To stay with our subject, we might define the various vocal styles developed during the history of western classical music as products of the evolution of the two planes so far identified (*language* and *sound*) and the evolution of their *intersection*.

Determining factors in this evolution are the acoustic and linguistic nature of the geographical site where a certain vocal style was born, the social (or religious) function of its singers, and their *status*. In the birth and evolution of a vocal *genre*, let it not be forgotten that migrations from outside are important, for they have contaminated languages with their various frequency bands[24], and, in consequence, with their relative cultures,

---

[24] «Differentiation between languages depends neither on their nature nor on their "soul". It depends on certain factors such as the environment, the immediate surroundings, the sonic geography. Like wine: the vine may be the same, but according to the setting up of the vineyard, the wines will have a different appearance, taste or colour according to the earth, the exposition, the climate, the wine-making, etc. [....] We see how the frequencies change their bandwidth as these cross continents, regions. Even though using the same language, an Englishman expresses himself on the tip of his tongue while his American cousin speaks through his nose. [...] The first factor is bound up with the acoustic impedance of places and environments. The acoustic impedance corresponds to the minimum sound resistance in our surroundings. When someone starts to speak and gets ready to listen – for he is the first listener to his own speech – he introduces between himself and his own language a dimension, a preparation that is not measurable and which acts upon the verbal flow, on

modifying, together with their manner of "feeling" – that is, of *hearing* – also the mentality of peoples[25] : this is a phenomenon becoming even more evident the more one approaches the "popular" types of music, since the music that today we call *classical* – i.e. written and printed music, essentially – has always been prerogative of the few, and those few who could permit themselves the luxury of buying writing paper did not usually need to emigrate in order to make a living.

Furthermore, worldwide acoustics (public and private) have undergone enormous changes in the past two hundred years following the industrial revolutions, urbanization, the diffusion of electricity and therefore of the mass media, the gramophone record and, finally, *internet*. Man must assert his existence in the context of a pressure of sound ever louder and ever more present, which two hundred years ago would have probably driven any one of his ancestors mad. In other words, a singer, like a composer, is a product and an interpreter of his times, of his environment, and in his singing reverberates what he hears (or no longer hears) around him.

Here we shall restrict ourselves to listing some of the fundamental moments of this evolution (which, as we shall see, includes some historical repetition), touching lightly upon them and always following the theme of the interplay of the planes of sound and language that this little treatise is dealing with, describing them just as we know them from the musical scores that have come down to us.

---

his intonation. The latency time is rather significant in songs, in folksong, in the manner of storytelling. These local products direct us to the pre-linguistic rhythm of the language of which nothing is left, in a certain way, except the mordant upon which semantics are grafted, even though already latent in this background music.»; A. Tomatis, *Op. Cit.*

[25] It is very interesting to observe how, with the spread of *trap* through various nations, the different languages that adopt the *genre* are moulding themselves to fit the original metre of American rap, with more or less happy results: French, for example, lends itself better because the accent falls constantly on the final syllable and easily imitates English (which is why there is a large francophone production of this *genre* of music); Italian, on the other hand, comes out of it deformed, having to transform all paroxytone words (those carrying the accent on the penultimate syllable, which in Italian constitute the vast majority) that are placed at the end of a line, into oxytone words (carrying the accent on the last one). Yet, in this deformation process we can see the birth of a somewhat new language.

Gregorian chant

Sung prayer: choral, unaccompanied, in unison. Always keeping within the range of speech, in *religious* respect for the metre of the sacred text, it usually entrusts the dialogue part to the *tenor* (from the Latin verb *teneo* – "to keep": a *ribattuto* melody that *sustains* the chant) and it aspires towards the absolute in the *jubilus*, that is, in the cadential *vocalise* (often on the *Amen*).

Developed in those temples of silence, the medieval cathedrals and monasteries, Gregorian chant codified the *neume* (from the Greek noun *pneuma*, "breath") within the *diastematic* musical notation system (as we call it today), starting from the intuitive notation of the text of the *chironomia*, that is the manual gesture of the choral director.

From the School of Notre Dame to the Madrigal

The purity of Gregorian becomes contaminated as it spreads. The placid psalmody becomes interrupted by *coloriture*, unison becomes *counterpoint* both melodic and linguistic; popular tunes insinuate themselves or are *interpolated* into the *sacred hymns* and various new-born languages (known respectively as *d'oc*, *d'oïl* and *del sì*, according to the way of saying "yes" in the relative regions) take their place beside *Latin*, and these sometimes appear together in one and the same piece, each to a different voice. The skill of the poetic text is the basis and the bait for the musical composition, which emerges almost automatically out of it. Dante would write, for the last time in Latin, the treatise *De Vulgari Eloquentia* maintaining the superiority of the *volgare italico* ("Italian popular language") – which he would eventually establish.[26]

The poets' main goal was to affirm the superiority of their own language, even giving it priority over the artistic objective, for underlying political and therefore economic reasons related to the feeding of the arts themselves.[27] Together with and thanks to languages, in fact, National States were being drawn up, whose borders were conquered by pen-strokes in the *disputes* of

---

[26] «That a power exists that elevates it, is clearly to be seen. In fact, what greater power than the possibility of changing the human heart and making the man who says no say yes, and the man who says yes say no, as this common speech has done and is doing?»; Dante Alighieri, *De Vulgari Eloquentia.*,

[27] Corrado Veneziano, *Manuale di dizione, voce e respirazione*, BESA, 1999.

the *tournaments* in which *troubadours* and *poets* contended and refined that absolute formal perfection already anticipating the *dramma per musica* (Dante calls those in the Divina Commedia *Canti* and *Cantiche;* Petrarch's are called *Canzoni*).

Opera, plural noun

Orpheus, the demigod who descended into the infernal regions to defy the gods and death itself, and to win back his lost love, is a prelude to and symbol of the initiative of the middle-class man of the future[28]. The Man of Humanism or the Renaissance had never been more a *faber fortunae suae* ("builder of his own fortunes"), he no longer depends on God nor is he subject to any king, but he is a free *citizen*. With the simple intention of reviving the culture of Ancient Greece, the Florentine *Camerata dei Bardi* invented on paper the absolutely self-referential *genre* that it would call *Opera*, from the plural of the neutral Latin noun *opus*[29]. This use of a plural noun was meant to include the art of local craftsmen (those who today make up the heart of what we stamp *Made in Italy*) while sponsoring them through

---

[28] Jacques Attali: *"Bruits - Essai sur l'économie politique de la musique"*, Presses Universitaires de France, 1977.

[29] Ŏpŭs, -eris; neutral noun III declension:
1 (in general) work, employment, job;
2 work, work performance, in any field;
3 agricultural work;
4 construction, fortification;
5 forced labor;
6 literary work;
7 invoice processing, style or way of working;
8 hard work, effort, labor;
9 action, activity, undertaking;
10 effect, outcome;
11 (in general) work accomplished, the product of a job;
12 construction, building;
13 rampart, trench, fortification or defense, siege engine;
14 dam embankment;
15 artwork;
16 literary genre;
17 clerical work superhuman, divine creation;
18 task, task, office, function;
19 (poetic) sexual intercourse.

this very peculiar, multifaced prototype of modern media advertising that was Opera.

However, the Camerata essentially founded the *genre* upon the musical qualities of the Italian language, which had to be promoted, exported, spread. The birth of Opera contributed, over the centuries, to the diffusion of the Italian language in a way that can only be compared with the arrival of radio and television in modern times.

Belcanto

The syllabic singing fashioned on the language of the first Opera, as had happened earlier with Gregorian chant, got broken up: the means was still the clarity and beauty of the words, but with the social elevation and increased power of the singers this ideal passed into second place leaving the spotlight on the naked vowel and the *vocalizzo*,

Treatises on singing are written and diffused (Giambattista Mancini, Manuel Garcia *Jr*) to formalize the study of the art. A *story-telling* in music is no longer the central need, but rather vocal prowess itself, exaggerated and used to delineate the character in an abstract fashion, through the *coloratura* (think of the *mad scenes*). Even though they are still too far away from the solutions offered by psychoanalysis, Rossini's neuroses express themselves through stuttering and onomatopoeia, in a way that already heralded the nineteenth-century's dissolution of language.

Lied

The intimist spirit of the bourgeois German let loose his *Sehnsucht* ("yearning") in the *Lied*, weaving it into the language of the great German national poets (above all, Goethe), setting it to music and spreading it through drawing rooms, thanks to the invention of the *pianoforte*. The heroic and at the same time melancholy art of Schubert, Schumann and Brahms would develop, in the Late Romantic period, into an orchestral format with Strauss and Mahler.

Parola scenica[30]

In the second half of the nineteenth century, the *volgare illustre* (Dante's *illustrious vernacular* – mentioned above) was destined to be intensively circulated in the newly-born Italy, and making it heard and sung, accompanied by bands on festal occasions, was a capital way of helping this along (Verdi's music was often accused of recalling a military band, or even hinting at the peasant's spade, but we no longer consider this an insult). The pragmatic Busseto peasant used to repeat to himself over and over again the lyrics sent to him by his librettists (with whom he usually engaged in an obsessive correspondence) until they began to burst into music spontaneously. This was the birth of the truest *musical dramaturgy* as we understand it today: due attention is paid to *action*, so the sung word must condense in one, two or three lemmata the entire dramatic *situation* and *position*[31], and make them clear to the spectator.

Verismo

Representation and Stylization are no longer enough. We are getting ever nearer to reality in cinema (then TV, then *reality shows*, and today *live streaming* from wherever something is happening), as near as we were to the drama of the two World Wars. In the midst of this second industrial revolution, the human voice must dominate huge orchestras and interpret destinies ever more inhuman and cruel; and what does it matter if this takes place in convents, houses or on the streets, among the hovels of the desperate.

Sprechgesang

The *too human*, or, frankly, inhuman destiny of twentieth-century man, and the existential disorientation that it gives rise to, is expressed thus in the heart of the world-wide upheaval of war. "God is dead", and so is *legato* (which significantly shares its etymon with the word *re-ligio*). Where language can no longer achieve the expression of a too ineffable sorrow and

---

[30] Verdi used this expression to define a word, or a small group of words, that synthetized and described the action and general situation taking place on the stage.

[31] "*Le parole della musica - Studi sulla lingua della letteratura musicale in onore di Gianfranco Folena*", LEO S. OLSCHKI, Florence, 1994.

the soul can sing no more, the word can no longer model or express: as soon as it is uttered, every syllable is abandoned to its fate, unable to last long enough to bind with the following one and to weave a melody.

Meta-language

The work of the artistic avant-garde and of some writers (above all, James Joyce), together with the advent of *psychoanalysis* (in particular Freud's studies of *lapsus linguae* – the "slips of the tongue" – and, in general, on the linguistics of dreams) have definitively transformed the concept of language. From a certain point of the XX century onwards, western composers have begun to abandon well-known languages, often making use of the phonetic symbols of the IPA[32] to ask the singer for a certain, specific *phoneme* rather than another, leaving any linguistic meaning out of the question, or even deliberately repudiating this. They treat the *signifiers* as sound objects complete in themselves, like multi-dimensional sensorial portals, that open the way to an experimentation also greatly encouraged by the advent of electronic music.

This has been the fundamental contribution made to vocal music by such composers as Berio, Scelsi, Cage, Bussotti, Kurtàg, Sciarrino, and Feldman – among others.

---

[32] International Phonetic Alphabet.

III. Raw material

First of all, therefore, I shall explain what I mean when I use the term 'illustrious', and why it is applied to the vulgar. Now when we call something 'illustrious', we mean that it gives off light and that, if struck by the light, it shines.

Dante Alighieri,
De Vulgari Eloquentia

Seven volumes of light and shade: *chiaroscuro*

Just as light is reflected and refracted in different ways by different surfaces, the voice, right from our first birth-cry, also encounters, to give it shape, different *vowel volumes* and, through these – in their composition, association and articulation – it acquires meanings, pace, colours, emotions. All known languages consist of *vowels* and *consonants*: the former, so called because it is through them that the *voice* is reflected and diffused, are *forms*, physical volumes that take life from the laryngeal sound; the latter are nothing more than mute spasms of the face and tongue, accessory muscular attitudes that *con-sonano* ("sound together") with the vowels, endowing discourse with form and rhythm.

Tomatis explains[33] how in all the world's languages each vowel has its own specific *volume*, which remains intact at any frequency at which it is intoned, reminding us at the same time how, conversely, not all the vocalic volumes produced by man necessarily correspond to recognized vowels in any language.

The Italian language is extremely selective in this regard: the vocalic volumes included in it are few in comparison with, for example, the more than twenty of English or the seventeen of Swedish. Such selectivity allows us to realize that these few volumes are, on the other hand, quite enough to express all the emotional and semantic range and that they have, therefore, a great intrinsic value, in their *simplicity* (in the etymological sense of "without folds";

---

[33] From *The Ear and the Voice* by A. Tomatis.

that is *simple* as the opposite of *multiple*[34]). Such an intrinsic value may be attributed to their *musical* potential.

The Italian alphabet contains, in fact, only *five graphemes* indicating vowel sounds: this number, however, does not correspond to the actual number of vowels spoken. Three of these five graphemes, in fact – *a, i, u* – can only be pronounced in one way, each corresponding to one sound only; the other two graphemes, on the other hand – *e, o* – offer two different options of pronunciation each (this *only if they are found in the tonic position*: if *atonic*, or weak, they are called closed by *default*, as we shall see better later). In this way the oral Italian vowels are no longer five, as in writing, but seven: *a*, open *e*, closed *e*, *i*, open *o*, closed *o*, *u*. This orthographic omission from the Italian alphabet[35], as we shall understand more fully later on, is not lacking in importance, in particular as regards singing. Here we have decided to remedy matters as follows:

> We shall opt for the symbols **æ** and **ɶ** to write the *open e* and *o*, for reasons concerning vocal technique which we will illustrate later.
> The symbols **e** and **o** will stand from here on for the closed version of the same vowels.

The *seven Italian vowels* will therefore be for us, in alphabetical order of appearance:

    1. a   **2. æ**   **3. e**   **4. i**   **5. ɶ**   **6. o**   **7. u**

---

[34] From the *Vocabolario Treccani* online: «**sémplice** (archaic **sìmplice**) adj. [Latin *simplex simplicis*, root *sem-* 'one, one only' (c.f. *semel*] and of a root *plek-* present in *plectere* 'to lace up', *plicare* 'to fold' (c.f. *duplice, triplice…molteplice*)]. - 1. Consisting of one sole element and cannot therefore add other components […] In further cases, always in direct or indirect contrast with *composite*, it means that it is not mixed or combined with anything else) […] "*Aristotle proposes, as we have said, simple movements and mixed movement, giving the name simple to the circle and the line, and mixed an amalgamation of these two."* (G. Galilei).».

[35] Omission probably due to differences in pronunciation of the vowels between different regional dialects when the language began to spread (which happened very recently: the advent of the media has permitted the configuration of a standard Italian, which, however, remains defective and needing revision in spelling).

These are *seven pure vocalic volumes,* which are *unmoving* and, as before, *simple*: that is, while they are being enunciated they undergo no change, nor are they affected by neighboring sounds – as happens in other languages. That is because they offer a minimum *muscular impedance* while they are being produced and they have a sufficiently short latent period[36] and a comfortable position with respect to the larynx[37]. They turn out to be easily obtainable and "comfortable", truly *singable*. Seven perfect forms, so much so as to be defined *archetypes* by Juvarra[38].

Not by chance, through an established convention due to acoustic-linguistic reasons, in the singing of the western cultured world it is common to assimilate the sung vowels of any foreign language to the Italian ones.

> In whatever language one is preparing to sing, in fact, a singer will warm up his voice vocalizing on the Italian vowels.

(The same may be said for certain consonants: for example the *r* of French, English and German, which in Opera is usually drawn near to the Italian pronunciation, for, unlike all the others, it does not disturb or "displace" the vocal emission).

---

[36] «Between the moment when the ear begins to listen and that in which the sound that it is expecting is made manifest, the time of latency is established [....] It is not well-known, but it presupposes a preparation on the part of the body, the ear, and the nervous system. I have succeeded in measuring it above all through the attack of the sound, while I was studying the behavior of opera singers.»; A. Tomatis, *Siamo tutti nati poliglotti*, IBIS, 2003.

[37] Tomatis, *Op. Cit.*, on the positioning of the larynx in various languages: «Thanks to the sophisticated apparatuses available to us today, I have been able to achieve precise measurements, close to 50 thousandths of a second. The English and the Spanish share the first prize for speed with 5 thousandths of a second. This performance is facilitated for the Spanish who speak very near to the base of the larynx. For the English this is a tour de force, their listening curve forces them to speak on the tip of the tongue, more than 16 centimeters away from the larynx. They are subjected to constant pressure and suffer terribly in the effort to speak so quickly – which is doubtless the cause of their affected and slightly hesitant air.»

[38] A. Juvarra, "*Figure dell'immaginario vocale*" and "*Manuel Garcia Jr*" both published on the blog *Mozart 2006*, respectively in June 2016 and June 2018.

The circle

All the celebrated singers of the past knew from experience that the so-called Italian vowels A, E, I, O, U [39] (or rather, the five vowels as conceived and pronounced by the Italians) constitute the true basis of voice and singing, that is, of Belcanto.
They all knew that, in order to sing well, a sound knowledge of Italian is indispensable – that is, a knowledge of the language as spoken by the Italians themselves, a language that knows no other vowel sounds than the above mentioned (and of course modifications thereof), that has no nasal, no guttural, and no harsh sounds whatever.
The Italian talks with these five vowels both in their purest form, and with slight modifications thereof for the purposes of greater expression and accentuation, according to circumstances. Furthermore, the Italian's conception of these five vowels in relation to his own spoken language demands imperatively that they be produced on a clear and flowing basis.
A good Italian singer – a product of the real School, one and only, speaks as he sings for the very reason that basically he expresses himself mainly with the aforesaid five pure fluid vowels, which for convenience sake are called Italian, or classic, but which as a matter of fact are found in practically every language of civilized and uncivilized peoples, although not always, or shall we say rarely, if at all, under the same purity of form and colour and accentuation as known to the Italian".

Beniamino Gigli,
Introductory lesson to Herbert Caesari's "Voice of the Mind"

As part of the practical intentions of this treatise, it is proposed to reconsider not only the spelling of the vowels in the Italian alphabet, but also their order of appearance within it. These seven vowels are, in fact, extraordinarily close to one another and consequential to each other in diction, if they are arranged in an order other than the alphabetical one, as we will now show.

---

[39] See note 35.

Let us consider the vowel *a* as a *matrix*[40] – a sort of gravitational pole of the open position. From this matrix two variants branch off and can be distinguished, one more rarified – *æ* – and another, more dense – *ɑɒ*.[41]

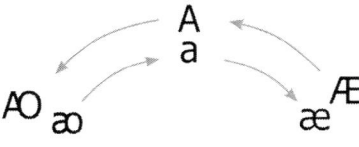

Fig. 1

Consequently, the vowels nearest to the open *æ* and the open *ɑɒ* will be their respective, closed homographs: *e, o*:

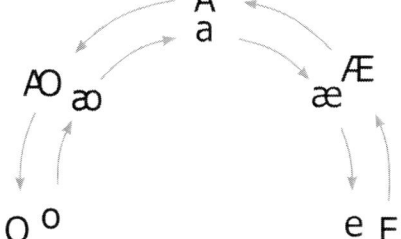

Fig. 2

Finally, *o* and *u* are contiguous because they are "sister" vowels, often constituting interchangeable alternatives in languages that are neighbors either in space (like Italian and French) or in time (like Italian and Latin), if found within the sphere of one and the same etymon; furthermore, in many languages the sound of the Italian *u* can be obtained writing "ou" or "oo".

The same may be said for the consequentiality between *u* and *i*, since in many languages their pronunciation is extremely similar (the French *u* is almost an Italian *i*, and so is the German ü).

---

[40] In almost all alphabets, including the Italian, the *alpha* -A- is drawn as an open mouth, a triangle (with its vertex at the top or at the side and open on the opposite side). The grapheme is also thought to descend from a stylized bull's head derived from the constellation of Taurus, the one that opens spring and is therefore the appropriate symbol of a primigenial sound.

[41] Not by chance we speak here of more *rarefied* or *densified vowels*, instead of *clear* and *dark* ones, to avoid confusion: an *æ* may be as rarified as it is dark at the same time (for instance, when we sing of the *dì estræmo*; in the same way an *ɑɒ* may be as dense as it is sunny (in *un mɑɒto di giɑɒya*).

Idem for *i* and *e* (ex.: Lat. *intra* → It. *e*ntro, Lat. *video* → It. v*e*do; Eng. *pain, (to) pine, pen, pin* → It. p*e*na, struggersi, p*e*nna, p*i*nna). This is why we complete our design thus; and, as the arrows suggest, this circle can be read both clockwise and counterclockwise:

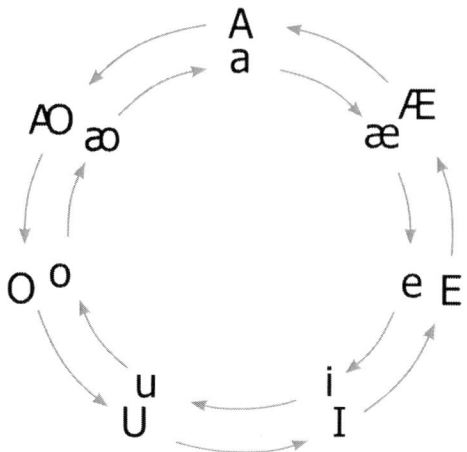

Fig. 3

Fundamental vowel exercise

In order to verify the consequentiality of this circular order, you may now try to say aloud – repeatedly and absolutely *legato*, in other words *never* breaking the flow of the sound-line – the two following *vocalic octaves*, which correspond to the *perimeter of the circle* pictured above, running through it in both directions.

That is, clockwise: **a_æ_e_i_u_o_ɒ_a**

and, anti-clockwise: **a_ɒ_o_u_i_e_æ_a**

If the exercise is done well, a perfect *circularity of aperture* will be observed, even in the movement of the mouth.[42]

> **The student is invited to concentrate on this exercise, especially in its most basic form (fig. 3), for, if well performed, it is of such importance as to constitute an *excellent* foundation for warming up and for the daily training of the singer for the rest of his vocal life.**

---

[42] Think of words like *aiuola* ("flower bed") or *aureola*, which describe circular concepts and, in pronunciation – this too describing a circle with the mouth – embrace all the volumetric apertures here illustrated.

We have begun the octave from the vowel *a* merely from an alphabetical principle; now do the same exercise again, but beginning the octave from any other vowel, just as you like, still maintaining, however, the consequential order indicated above, also in the anti-clockwise motion.

For example, beginning with the *i*, we get: **i_u_o_ɒ_a_æ_e_i**

and then, going backwards,   **i_e_æ_a_ɒ_o_u_i**

Beginning with the *o*, we get: **o_ɒ_a_æ_e_i_u_o**

and backwards: **o_u_i_e_æ_a_ɒ_o**,

etcetera.

> **N.B.:** First be sure to *understand*, and consequently memorize, the illustrated order of the vowels in the circle, until you have completely mastered it, so as to be able to use it to practice the fundamental exercise of Italian vocalization, beginning with *any one* of the seven vowels, at will, continuing in both directions: clockwise and anti-clockwise.

The reader may progressively develop and vary this basic exercise, passing from a *parlato appoggiato* ("supported speaking") to a sort of *chanting* on one note, and then on to a real vocalize, which will first dwell on long sustained notes and then accelerate, beginning with elementary intervals until at last he arrives at short scales, arpeggios or extemporized melodies suited to the repertoire envisaged.

Italian: malleable, but *untouchable*

The vocalic volumes of Italian, when they are "lit up" by the vocal sound, produce a particular halo, a "mist" which *binds* each sound to the preceding and the succeeding one, creating in this way a *vocal line* which is perceived as continuous in its fluidity of emission (rather what happens in the case of our *Milky Way*, which the human eye sees as a *continuum,* even though it is made up of myriads of individual stars, but to our eyes "bound" one to another by the milky blaze that they emanate). This continuous flow of measured sound, that is born from speaking and singing on the Italian vowels, and called *legato* (which means, precisely, *bound)*, is perhaps the principal characteristic of the "cultured" western sound, first of all, vocal, and then, by extension, also instrumental.

There are languages in which sung vowels, because of the consonantal borders confining them and the *time of latency*[43] characterizing them, are comparable to sealed *packages* – separated from each other and each filled with its own sound – which then get placed one after another in speaking and singing, but in such a way that each element of the series remains isolated and confined. In Italian things go very differently. Italian – especially sung Italian, which is a *spacetime macroscopy* of spoken Italian – is one continuous, uninterrupted flow of *vocal fluidity* which finds itself accompanied, caressingly mirrored in, lovingly welcomed and only illusorily reflected by vocalic volumes that are nothing but abstract forms, projections of the mind, always separated from vocal emission, that is, from the undulatory source, from the source of the sound wave, from the laryngeal *vibrator*. In other words, the language of Italy, like its visible and (more) tangible masterpieces in museums, is *not to be touched*. The penalty would be that its crystalline *transparency*[44] might be soiled and that its power of refracting the voice might be compromised, a power thanks to which the language can release its peculiar *legato* (so called also because it binds man to *everything* through the enchantments of the Muse). Italian, therefore, must not be either *managed* or *manipulated* – or rather *chewed* – with the muscles of the phonatory apparatus – ever. (The Italian language and a good vocal technique enable the singer to suggest the look of a Madonna of Raphael's, when singing, and to assume the relaxed and enigmatic facial posture of the Leonardo type.)

In music the opposite of *legato* is the *staccato,* which may derive aesthetically from the neatness of the pronunciation of the *double consonants* of Italian and of its *syntactic germination,* which we shall describe in the following chapter.

---

[43] See notes 36 and 37.

[44] See the quote from Massimo Mila, on page 9.

It is due to these intrinsic characteristics of our language – to its neat dichotomies, to the *chiaroscuro* [45] of its alternation of open and closed vowels and the roundness of them all, to the *rhythm* of the double consonants, which enlivens the placid continuity of the vowels – the fact that it gave birth to one of the maximum expressions of singing – Opera – and also that the international lexicon of classical music is Italian. Our essentially binary way of talking is characterized by its dramatic alternations: *legato/staccato*, *piano/forte*, *crescendo/diminuendo*, *adagio/presto* etc.

In Italian, in other words, what is not *open* is *closed* and what is not wide is narrow – period. This binary system, comparable to the *0-1* of computer programs, in its dichotomous simplicity, designs and paints: it creates perspectives, depths, heights and valleys, portraits, choral scenes, universes.

The accents

In archaic Italian, as well as in the operatic kind, the synecdoche *accenti*[46] ("accents") is sometimes used to mean *words,* showing the importance that accents came to have in poetry and how the tonic vowels made all the other syllables of the verse gravitate around them, making every word a *parabola* (this is the etymon of the lemma) describing with its equation a specific *moto* ("motion")[47] either ascending or descending, reaching its climax and then, at last, coming down. (Let us point out that within every word of three or more syllables there are, besides the one principal accent, some *secondary*

---

[45] The Italian language, in other words, is malleable and puts the vocalic volumes in the limelight: it was precisely thanks to his mastery of the *chiaroscuro* concept and technique that Galileo – lutenist and physicist, son of the very Vincenzo Galilei of the Camerata dei Bardi who, in fact, invented Opera – succeeded in intuiting the existence of lunar craters and designed them with absolute precision: it is difficult not to think that the scientist's predisposition to this binary kind of thinking, combined with the greatest sense of the practical (his father brought him up experimenting on the cords of the lute), were inherited from the national genius and in particular from the mother tongue, apart from his being in addition an accomplished musician (Einstein also intuited the curvature of space time while playing the violin).

[46] «The *Greek* word prosodia – from *pros* (in Lat. "ad", "towards, for") and *odè* (in Lat. "cantus", "weight" but also "resonance") – was rendered into Latin by the expression *ad cantum*, from which we get *accentus*. The Greek term signified raising the voice to pronounce the stressed syllable; then it indicated the duration of pronunciation in the body of the word; then, finally, it meant the collection of rules and precepts that teach us the quantities of the syllables composing the word.»; Enrico Di Marzo, *Prosodia e Metrica Latina*, Paravia 1946.

[47] In archaic Italian, "word" was also *motto*, as the modern French *mot*.

accents that, although important to the malleability of the verse, are not dealt with here, because they do not affect diction.)

The *quantitative metric*, typical of the prosody in classical languages like Latin and Greek and consisting in the regulated succession of prearranged *long vowels* with *short vowels* within an equally prearranged poetic verse, became progressively obsolete with the advent of *musical notation*: thanks to the latter, in fact, it was no longer necessary to establish a linguistic metre in order to fix the musical rhythm of the verse, this being made recognizable by the emptiness or fullness of notes and finally by a numerical fraction placed at the head of the line of music (for the speed we have always resorted to verbal locutions: *ad agio, allegro, presto, andante*). In the Romance languages, including Italian, they passed therefore from a *quantitive* metric to an *accentual* metric, based on the singling out of *just one* strong or *tonic* vowel within each word, which is the one bearing the *accent*.

All of the others are, automatically, considered weak or *atonal* (that is, without *tone*, without *sound*: to be made little of, in other words)[48].

According to where their *only* tonic accent falls, we classify words as:

---

[48] From the *Enciclopedia Treccani* online, at the entry "sillaba": «Syllables ending in a vowel are called *aperte* ("open") or *libere* ("free")" (e.g. the three syllables of *pa-ga-re*); those ending in a consonant are called *chiuse* ("closed") or *implicate* ("involved") (e.g. the first two of *con-trat-to*). In many languages the *freedom* or *involvement* of the syllables determines the quantity, mechanical and not distinctive, of their respective vowels: it often happens that the vowels of the open syllables are long, those of the closed syllables are short. This approximate rule has also a partial application in Italian: an Italian vowel is, in fact, long on condition that it is tonic and ending a syllable (or, in an open syllable) but not a word (e.g. the *a* of *fato*), as all the atonal vowels are short, those that do not end a syllable (or, in a closed syllable) and those that end a word (e.g. the *a* of *fatidico*, of *fatto*, of *fa*).

Italian Definition	English Definition	Meaning	Examples
Tronche	Oxytone	Carrying the tonic accent on their last or only syllable	*perché, è, dà, né, però, beltà, virtù, andrò, testè, così, etc.*
Piane	Paroxytone	Carrying the tonic accent on their penultimate syllable (constituting the vast majority of Italian words)	*andiamo, piano, forte, adagio, bello, mio, semplicemente, davvero, ecco, etc.*
Sdrucciole	Proparoxytone	Carrying the tonic accent on their antepenultimate syllable.	*seggiola, manico, ultimo, unico, leggere, mandorla, albero, ottimo, palpito, dammelo, guardami, etc.*
Bisdrucciole	/	Carrying the tonic accent on their preantepenultimate syllable (they can only be verbal forms associated with pronouns).	*andiamocene, portaglielo, donatemelo, diciamocelo, conservatelo, etc.*

The spaces of the vocalic volumes

In the pronunciation of Italian vowels we can enumerate *two phonatory positions*, one *wide* and the other more *circumscribed* or *narrow* (but never *tight!*) according to whether the tongue, during the phonatory act, is respectively nearer to or farther from the palate.

> **Important**: if in this text we do not use demonstrative illustrations of the vocal apparatus of how to position the mouth in enunciating, it is because, depending on the physiognomy and conformation of each singer, there is no common position of the mouth or tongue by means of which everybody should follow the one right phonetic objective; quite the reverse: the correct *covering* of the sound (the reader is referred to page 29 - 30) would completely defeat our efforts to find one.

We use the term *wide* for those vowels that dwell in the same ideal space occupied by our most comfortable *a*, as exclaimed in a satisfying sigh of relief: "*Ah!*".

In the wide position all the throat is completely relaxed, and so is the jaw (which should be hanging completely loose) and also the tongue[49] (which should be lying asleep as if the dentist had anesthetized it and we could not even flex it enough to be able to speak).

The vowels occupying the wide position are three:

1. *a* (*aria* → a̲ria);
2. *æ* (*ecco* → æ̲cco, *sedia* → sæ̲dia, *cesto* → cæ̲sto, *esperto* → espæ̲rto, *tè* → tæ̲);
3. *ɑ̲o* (*oggi* → ɑ̲oggi, *accolgo* → accɑ̲olgo, *nonna* → nɑ̲onna, *andò* → andɑ̲o).

---

[49] The tenor Franco Corelli was famous for the complete relaxation of his oral cavity while singing, to the extent of sounding as if he had a speech impediment (which he had not, as witnessed by the recordings of his interviews).

> The choice we have made, here, of graphically assimilating all the wide vowels to their matrix, aims at making the singer's pronunciation intuitive, so that he avoids modifying in any way the arrangement of his face and vocal instrument while passing from his best and most comfortable *a* to the other two deriving from it, in particular forbidding his tongue to stiffen or make any conscious action, while at the same time making sure that the three vowels are clearly distinguishable by the ear.

As an exercise, pronounce these three vowels one after the other, alternating them in whatever order you like, keeping to speech mode and on one continuous note, and observing, we repeat, the *maximum* degree of relaxation of the muscles of the face, tongue, jaw and neck. Make sure, in passing from one to another, that no changes take place, unless they are unavoidable and almost *unnoticeable*, in the arrangement of the face: to obtain these three different *nuances* of the wide position all that will be necessary is a gentle positioning of the tongue in response to the variations in the requests from the brain and the ear – a response that you do *not* need to be consciously aware of, it is sufficient to let it happen without intervening.

Try and chant, then, sustaining each vowel: "**a_æ_a_ɶ_æ_a...**" etc.

Once you have got familiar with these three forms, you can start transposing the exercise onto different notes, which at first you may keep approximate (rather than tune them precisely and therefore worry about keeping them in tune, in the beginning you should limit yourself to "gravitating" around a comfortable pitch) and then gradually increase precision (singing little melodic intervals, short scales, always *ad agio*).

> **N.B.** While exercising, never judge the *vocal* quality of the sound emitted, but only its *vocalic* quality, which should be sought *first* in the mind and *then* with the ear (but never, *never* with a muscular manipulation of the mouth, tongue or throat, for this would endanger or ruin the legato), until what you hear – in colour, elegance and linguistic accuracy – comes to coincide with what you had previously envisioned.

A vowel is *circumscribed* or *narrow* if it dwells in the same ideal space as the Italian *i*, which is the antipodes of the *a*, as we have seen, in the synoptic circle.

The vowels in the circumscribed position are the four remaining:

1. *o* closed (*ora*);   **2. *u*** (*uno*)   **3. i** (*io*);   **4. *e*** closed (*entro*).

Proceed by exercising these vowels as you have just done for the wide vowels, in their consequential and not alphabetical order, as suggested above: o _ u _ i _ e

also backwards: e _ i _ u _ o.

The vocalic volumes, if they are obtained exclusively by ear and without any muscular effort, will already, in themselves, guarantee an aesthetic victory for the sound, which will fix itself in place. (It will probably happen that, for some singers whose hearing has been falsified, it will be difficult initially to accustom the ear to this simplicity of emission.)

But what spaces are occupied by the *atonic vowels?*

Since their objective is certainly that of filling in the vocal line, but without drawing too much attention to themselves (that is without hatching accents that might go to undermine the priority of the main accent):

> **the atonic vowels must never be opened.**

We say "must never be opened" instead of "must be closed" because we shall not spend time or insist on closing *atonic* vowels with the same energy that we devote to closing the *tonic* vowels: it will be enough to keep the atonic ones circumscribed, not to open them nor deform them, match them to the vocal line, let them flow forth without disturbing the phrase.

We shall further discuss their orthoepical treatment in the next chapter, dealing with the rules of diction.

Let *nothing* have its say

In the International Phonetic Alphabet there is a vowel called *schwa* ("nothing", in Hebrew) and it is represented by the grapheme ə. This is one of the most omnipresent vowels in all the languages of the world and, something perhaps less well known, it is present in Italian, too. To make it clear, this is the vowel used in pronouncing the English article *the*: it has also always turned up in Italian diction and, furthermore, has only recently lost its corresponding letter in the Italian alphabet, which indicated it by the letter *j* (a grapheme in Italian indicating an *i lunga,* a "long i", meaning an *i* protracted in time – in words such as *noja, gioja, ajuto, cuojo*[50] – until at least the 'forties of the XX century; Opera libretti, furthermore, are chock-full of them). Although today it has been assimilated into the *i* in writing through a crude approximation in sound and orthography, it is still pronounced and heard in an unmistakably different way; for example, in diphthongs (we pronounce *figlio* as → fi̱llǝo[51], in fact, and not → fi̱glio[52]).

In the context of this present manual, this vowel interests us not so much on the linguistic or historical side, but for its *technical-vocal qualities*, because we need to know how to let it cunningly infiltrate, where necessary, with the aim of maintaining the vocal line and its *legato* intact, whenever these might risk being broken up by the tricks played by conglomerations of consonants, or also with the aim of underlining, for interpretative reasons, the internal consonants of the word. Quite differently from German, for example, where to reinforce a word one goes straight to its initial consonant, in Italian one

---

[50] Today it would correspond more to the sound of a *y* in words like *yoga* and *yogurt.*
[51] See paragraph "How to notate diction" on page 61.
[52] We point out that Treccani uses, for the group *gli/glie* the sign for the Greek *lambda*: *figlio* /ˈfiʎo/.

may and one must do this with the intermediate ones, if no obligatory syntactic germination is required on the initial consonant: and this is how, if necessary, *sprezzo* could become /səpərrǣzzo/; *crudele* would come out as /kərrudǣle/, and so on.

For the business of singing we might also, in addition, distinguish between a wider *schwa* (that we may notate as *ɜ*) and a more circumscribed one (*ə*). The difference in pronunciation between the two would lie only in the different distance of the tongue from the palate (we will pronounce the wider version as an *ə* ideally overlapped by an *a*, and the narrow version as an *ə* overlapped by an *i*): when singing, we shall choose on each occasion the one most adapted to our need, depending on whether it must follow, anticipate or conjoin vowels either open or closed.

Here the author intends to forestall the objection of any reader who might consider the use of this vowel to be antiquated or affected: this is by no means the case. Spoken Italian is, in fact, full of it; only the Italian language – unlike all other languages – is not accustomed to *codifying* this vocalic sound, just because it lacks any corresponding *orthographic* representation, and so deems it superseded, or indeed *non-existent*. But what amounts to a mere absence from our alphabet (and not the only one, nor the most serious) cannot be allowed to become ignorance of a *fact*, especially in singing and its teaching. It is opportune to bear in mind that, especially for the non-Italian ear (and pupil):

**the schwa is a vowel exactly like all the others,
which absolutely must be identified, acknowledged, dealt with;
and _written_.**

So much so that we will integrate our circle as follows:[53]

Finally, it will be the good *teacher's* task to teach how to use it where necessary in singing, allowing it to pass unobserved in *legato*, just as it does in speech. On condition that it is adopted as it should be, with taste and *with a grain of salt*, the potential objection raised above is firmly rejected.

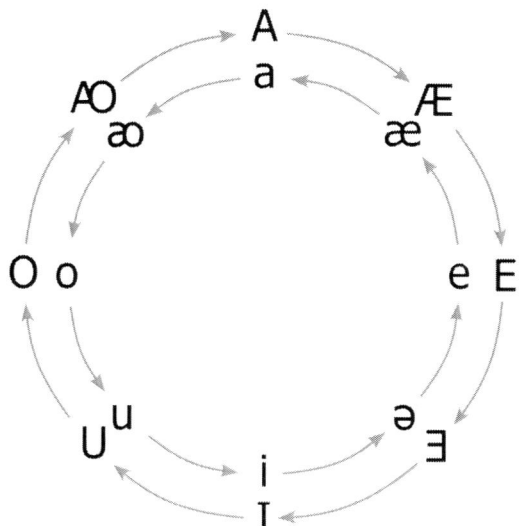

Fig. 4

Synopsis

Up to here we have counted all the vocalic sounds in the Italian language, coming up with eight:

- ✓ three wide ones: **a, æ, ɒ;**
- ✓ four narrow ones: **o, u, i, e;**
- ✓ one polyvalent *passepartout*: **ə.**

The singer will first practice them with *legato* in the circular order already suggested (try and *chant* them): **a‿æ‿e‿i‿u‿o‿ɒ‿a,**

also backwards (try and *chant* them): **a‿ɒ‿o‿u‿i‿e‿æ‿a,**

in order to memorize it and help himself to differentiate vocalic volumes from those near them. This order has also, in fact, the virtue of relativizing these apertures one to another, forcing the singer to bring into focus the *subtle* differences between the adjacent ones and to learn above all to distinguish them with his own ears (this is by no means negligible: very many cannot distinguish an open vowel from its closed homologue, and quite often struggle to differentiate between an *i* and a closed *e*, or a *u* and a closed *o*).

---

[53] In this drawing we placed the schwa between the *e* and the *i* for mere reasons of visual symmetry, not of consequentiality.

Once he has acquired a good mastery of the volumes in the order indicated, the singer may amuse himself by pronouncing them, one after another as before, but changing the order and, this time, interposing them with the *schwa*, both in its wide and its narrow form, as he likes:

…i_o_ə_æ_ə_u_ə_i_a_ə_ɶ…

Repeat this chanting, first of all on the same, sustained note – or better, gravitating around one note, in the medium-low speech register – then later venture on comfortable little intervals or little scales as you fancy, however *without concentrating on the intonation, which must not dominate, in case it compromises the accuracy of the vowels*: remember that we are dealing with abstract volumes and as such your *mental image* of them does not vary if the note happens to vary.

> **N.B.** Do the exercise regularly ensuring the perfect imperturbability of the facial expression and physical stance, at the same time ascertaining that for the vowels, within each single exercise, the same *character* is always maintained, where for "character" we mean the *font* itself – we will use a visual metaphor in everyday use to describe it – taking care that it remains ideally always unchanged, of the same dimension, depth and colour.

Let this *font* be precisely the *font* of our sound, its ideal *source;* let us choose it mentally at the start and maintain it intact for the whole exercise, without ever deforming it through temporary lack of skill; let us give it time to *inform* us, in the sense of *giving us form.*

We must slowly inform and put together our own *vocalic technique* upon the acoustic-visual idea that we have of the volumes of the vowels, refining it all the time; we must be inspired by that idea constantly in singing and we must determine to remain ever absolutely faithful to it; we must have patience and not accept compromises: the result is guaranteed.

PART TWO
DICTION, PRACTICE, INTERPRETATION

IV. Rules

Italian diction is *simple* and *linear* (two etymologically homologous concepts, as we have seen, since that which is *without folds* can *draw a line*): if this were not so, as already pointed out, Italian would not have given birth to the *genre* dealt with in this treatise.[54] But at the same time it is something by no means *easy*, so much so that the great majority of singers, even Italian ones, are unfortunately far away from understanding it and even less from mastering it, and far from recognizing the importance it has as architect and host of the vocal line. In fact, correct diction implicates correct musical *phrasing* and, if respected, highlights the symmetry, the assonances and the *onomatopoeias* to which the librettist dedicates the utmost care[55], so that the listener can detect a structure, a design in the text, a *pattern* by which his ear can be satisfied and *enchanted*.

To sing Italian, or rather *to let the Italian language spontaneously sing*, it will be enough to satisfy certain basic principles that we shall try to list here below. But before going on, we should like to give the reader some practical instruments to enable him to put into practice what he has learned.

A fundamental step is to learn how to note down *orthoepy* – the correct way to enunciate every word – in a simple manner that will make studying easier.

How to notate diction

We have amply noted how, although in its spelling Italian tends to be faithful to the sound, there are some ambiguities and imprecisions in its orthography that deprive it of some of the potential valuable to singers. For this reason we suggest that in your studies you adopt the notation indicated below for

---

[54] See again the quote from Jacopo Peri's introduction to his *Euridice*, on page 11.

[55] «You tell me to have patience with the slowness of artistic work. The problem is that what I am doing to that libretto is not artistic work, but detailed pedantry, indispensable yet most exhausting. It is a job that absolutely has to be done, it is work that needs an artist, but it is a job that does not stimulate and has no internal warmth. Artistic work has its painful and laborious hours, but in compensation it has its hours of inspiration in which the hand can hardly follow the mind. Here there is nothing to raise my spirits. I can assure you that to such an undertaking, wanting to engage in it with a clear conscience, I would never sit down again, for any money on earth.»; Giuseppe Giacosa, letter to Giulio Ricordi, 2 October 1893.

the following sounds and groups, specifying that the suggested notation differs from the official one of the International Phonetic Alphabet, since it has been especially designed by the author of this manual for the singer's practical use in Italian operatic diction.

Vowels

One more time, we warmly recommend that you:

- ✓ **mark the only *tonic* vowel of every word simply by underlining it** – that is, without marking it with any accent – exactly as you have seen us do in the course of this treatise (d<u>e</u>ntro, s<u>æ</u>mpre, dappert<u>u</u>tto);

- ✓ **mark the open *e* and *o* exclusively by prefixing them with their matrix *a***, as you have seen us do here, and in *no* other way (*costa* → c<u>ao</u>sta; *festa* → f<u>æ</u>sta): where the eye does not catch the pencil mark of the additional *a* joined with the broad vowels deriving from it, the brain will *automatically* accustom itself to closing, maintaining a more stable vocal line, less subject to bumps, or to any attempts to manipulate or chew the sound;

- ✓ **do *not* mark the atonal vowels in *any* way**, thus getting used to mentally thinking of them automatically as *non-open*: since the open vowels are a very spare minority in comparison with the closed, and the tonic vowels are an even more spare minority in respect to the atonal, in this way you will have fewer markings on your score, markings neater and more essential, which will help both learning and memory.

Three triplets

The groups *sc*, *gl*, *gn* are to be considered in pronunciation on a par with the double consonants, but even stronger and more impeding to pronunciation: they are in fact the thickest *knots* that are to be encountered along the thread of the Italian tongue, so much so that, rather than *double*, we might well dub them *triple consonants*. A librettist always adopts them to balance the *doubles* in the line and they are pronounced, and therefore should be annotated, as follows):

- ✓ **sce**, **scio**, **scia** → **schə**e/**schə**æ, **schə**o/ **schə**ɶ, **schə**a (e.g.: scelgo → **schə**lgo; scena → **schə**æna, sciolgo → **schə**ɶlgo; poscia → pɶ**sschə**a; pescecane → pe**schə**cane);
- ✓ **gli**, **glie**, **glia**, **glio** → **llə**i, **llə**e/**llə**æ, **llə**a, **llə**o/**llə**ɶ (e.g.: figli → fi**llə**i; meglio → mæ**llə**o; biglietto → bi**llə**etto; medaglia → meda**llə**a);
- ✓ **gni**, **gne**, **gna**, **gno**, **gnu** → **nnə**i, **nnə**e/**nnə**æ, **nnə**a, **nnə**o/**nnə**ɶ, **nnə**u (e.g.: sogni → so**nnə**i; degne → de**nnə**e; bagnato → ba**nnə**ato; agnostico → a**nnə**ɶstico; ignudi → i**nnə**udi).

Ambiguous consonants

The following notation is recommended for these *ambiguous* consonants, that is consonants that are to be pronounced differently according to where and how they are placed (see the upcoming paragraph "Enunciation of the consonants"):

- ✓ **hard c** → **k** (e.g.: chiedo → **k**iedo; vecchio → væ**kk**io);
- ✓ **soft c** → **c** (certo → **c**ærto, bacio → ba**c**ə, accetta → a**cc**ætta; Cina → **C**ina);
- ✓ **soft g**, single → **dg** (getto → **dg**ætto) and double → **ddg** (aggiro → a**ddg**iro);
- ✓ **hard g** → **g** (gatto → **g**atto);
- ✓ **unvoiced s** → **s** (e.g.: sabbia → **s**abbia, assolto → a**ss**ɶlto);
- ✓ **voiced s** → **z** (e.g.: naso na**z**o);
- ✓ **unvoiced z**, singular → **ts** (e.g.: zampa → **ts**ampa; azione → a**ts**ione)[56] and double → **tts** (e.g.: pazzo → pa**tts**o);
- ✓ **voiced z**, singular → **dz**[57] (e.g.: zelo → **dz**ælo) and double → **ddz** (e.g.: azzardo → a**ddz**ardo).

---

[56] Truth to tell, an Italian always doubles this *z* there is no difference in intensity between the pronunciation of the *z* in *grazie* and in *pezzo*. The non-Italian singer is advised, however, to differ the notation between single and double because this instinctive identical pronunciation is not found in foreign singers.

[57] See the preceding note: the same observation might be made, but only if the voiced z is found as initial of the word.

Enunciation of vowels

Since three of the vowels in the Italian alphabet (*a, i, u*) can only be pronounced in one way and represent only themselves, it is only with the two remaining (*e, o*) that the only rule of diction of Italian vowels is concerned:

> **Each *e* and *o*, if in the tonic position, can potentially be sounded either open or closed**: therefore, in each individual case it is necessary to establish which is appropriate.

And how? The best, and the only one which we would advise, is that of looking up this information in any *orthoepic dictionary* (Treccani is always to be recommended, but there are many available on the web) which quotes the lemmata with their *tonic accent*: *grave* when it points down, indicating an open vowel (*bèllo* → bællo; *bòsco* → baosco), and *acute* when it points upwards, indicating a closed vowel (*béstia* → bestia; *bócca* → bocca).

If he has no dictionary, the singer could refer to his own knowledge, if any, of languages that are close to Italian (as said, either in time, like Latin, or in space, like French, for example, but the languages of the Saxon group are also useful), for the vocalic and orthographic mutations of a word between closely related languages can give him a hint towards diagnosing the closed or open nature of the tonic in question, with a good chance of a fairly successful result, because what is wide (or narrow) in one language, tends to be the same in another, for reasons of etymological communality.

Some examples[58]:

Close Languages	Italian	Etymon
LAT. *dulcis*	dolce	GR. *(d)glykos*

---

[58] He who has studied classics in his time will note, furthermore, that the vowels that were long in Latin will, in Italian, for the most part be closed vowels, for the closing of the vowel makes the sound of it more incisive and similar to a temporal lengthening in our perception.

Close Languages	**Italian**	**Etymon**
FR. *coeur*	c<u>ao</u>re	SSCR. *hrd*, GR. *kear*
LAT. *cælum*	cælo	GR. *koilos*
FR. *mort*	m<u>ao</u>rte	GOT. *maurthr*
ENG. *pin, pain*[59]	p<u>e</u>na, p<u>æ</u>nna, p<u>i</u>nna[60]	SSCR. *punya*
FR. *amour*	am<u>o</u>re	GR. *mao*
LAT. *rubius* FR. *rouge* TED. *rot*	r<u>o</u>sso	BRET. *rus*

These associations are not always valid, but often enough to run the risk of trying to make them when no more certain information is available on the spot.

You may also take into consideration whether the word includes a *suffix* or not, because this will behave always in the same way[61].

Yet, as we will never tire of repeating, it is always best to trust the dictionary: thanks to it, once one has better understood the etymon, the history, and the affiliations of the word in question and its relationship to other languages, it will be easier to imprint the pronunciation upon the memory in lasting form: even its interpretation in singing will be deeper and more meaningful.

With regard to the atonic vowels, all is soon told:

> **The atonic e and o should never stand out, therefore they are said short and closed.**

---

[59] The common root may indicate sharp, pointed or elongated shapes, or piercing feelings.

[60] See the preceding note.

[61] For example, the suffixes *-mento/ -mente* will always be closed (compim<u>e</u>nto, felicem<u>e</u>nte), the suffix *-enza* always open (pazi<u>æ</u>nza, dipend<u>æ</u>nza), *-ore* always closed (am<u>o</u>re, dol<u>o</u>re, col<u>o</u>re, stup<u>o</u>re), and so on.

And as the Italian language is made up on the whole of *parole piane*[62] ("paroxytone words", those carrying the accent on the penultimate syllable, the final one being therefore atonal) it goes without saying that:

> **The atonal *e* and *o* at the end of words must never be open.**

Take care: the fact that the atonal final vowels are *never open* does not mean synonymously that they must be meticulously *closed*. The trained ear detects a difference between a final vowel deliberately closed (which would be more evident, more tonic and more prolonged in time) and a vowel that is *atonal* and simply *not open* (shorter and less intense). The happy result of all this constant awareness will be a natural (and musical) *diminuendo* in the dynamics towards the final vowel, compared with the verbal area marked by the energy of the tonic accent, which will be automatically set in relief through an effect of perspective.

In respect to this generalized rule on the question of the *atonal final vowels*, a case apart are the *oxytone* words, the ones carrying their tonic accent on their last or only vowel (in Italian they are called *parole tronche* – "truncated words" – because they have lost a piece – an ending, a suffix, a final consonant– and have compensated for the loss with a written accent: *volontate → volontà; sic → sì, est → è*). In them the accent on the ending is expressly indicated, determining whether they should be pronounced *open* or *closed* (*però, perché, comò, testè, paltó*, etc.) according to whether the accent is acute or grave.

It is very important to point out that, in Italian:

> **monosyllabic forms are generally considered atonal**

and for this reason they are pronounced as such (metrically they lean on the following word, absorbing its tonic accent: se_dævi, ne_andiam, non_dirlo, col_sorriso, del_color, per_esæmpio, etc.).

---

[62] We are recalling the structural dichotomy of the language mentioned on page 49.

An exception to this last rule is made by:

- ✓ *monosyllabic verbs*, which cannot be considered atonal in that they too are words that were, to some extent, *truncated*, although without acquiring a written accent (*so* coming from *sapio*, *vo* from *vado*, *fo* from *faccio*);
- ✓ all the explicitly *accented monosyllabic forms* (*sì, ché, sé, né,* etc.);
- ✓ the negation *no* (pronounced open for the same reason, that is, the original truncation, deriving from the Latin *non* / *nonne*).

Note also that all *bisyllabic* words, if subject to *elision* (that is, losing their final vowel before another vowel: *posso io → poss'io*) turn themselves in fact into atonal monosyllables (*poss'*) and as such are pronounced closed (*p*a*osso io* but *poss'io*).

If the end vowel of a word coincides with the first vowel of the following word (*lascia almen)*, the two combine to form a *crasis*, in speech as in singing (*lascialmen*, instead of *lascia_almen*).

Vocalic *crowds*

And when, on the other hand, there are *two or more vowels* that are distinct and not assimilable, but *only one note* is given on which to sing them? That is, when the composer unites more than one vowel under a single note (as in the famous verse *"che farò senza Euridice"* in Gluck's aria[63], where the whole ***aeu*** cluster goes under just one note): what should we do in such cases? How should we deal with singing these vocalic clusters, and why?

The answers to these questions vary from case to case and depend on a wide range of factors: the speed of the musical tempo, the *verve* or the dramatic nature of the piece, the fact that the two vowels are within one and the same word (e.g.: *ombra mai fu*, in which the rapid vocalic mutation within the same one note on *mai* will have more or less the effect of the *quilisma* in Gregorian chant) or one of them is the final vowel of the preceding word while the other is the first of the succeeding one (*giunse_alfin il momento*), if they form a diphthong (*fiume*) or a hiatus (*mio*).

---

[63] C. W. Gluck, *Orfeo*, Act III.

There is no codified, unitary rule for any of these cases: priority should be given, with the help of a *coach*, to ensuring the greater length of whichever vowel carries the tonic accent, and, more generally, whatever guarantees the intelligibility of the text, highlighting any possible assonances with the vowels (or associations of vowels) surrounding the ones in question. Typically, the shortened vowel of the two will always come close to an indistinct *schwa*, if it is listened to as if "slowed down on playback" (which is, looked at under a magnifying glass). Sometimes one can eliminate one of them completely (think of Leonora's *Di tale amor che dirsi* [64], where the final *e* of *tale* can easily drop out without anybody noticing, given the tempo and the *staccato* writing). At other times one deliberately creates a hiatus in order to underline the meaning of the word, arbitrarily adding a little "ghost note" (think of Germont's *Piangi, piangi, o misera* [65], where the *pia* is on the same note: if we make a hiatus of *ia*, in order to better sculpt the *parola scenica*, we are actually going to sing two notes, one for each vowel, instead of the single one written).

In these cases the good taste of the singer and his grasp of the language will be decisive: Italian is scantily codified exactly because of its malleable and *poetic* nature: it was born, and remains, flexible and creative; *free*.

Enunciation of consonants

This paragraph is as essential as it is unnecessary, since we can find the information it contains in any kind of orthoepic dictionary, also online. Therefore, whoever does not possess the memory, or the patience, or the time to commit to memory the information about to be displayed below may jump this paragraph without feeling guilty.

As before, also in dealing with the consonants we shall not be offering information that cannot be gleaned in better and more exhaustive form elsewhere: we recommend whoever would like more detailed information on the linguistic and theoretical aspect of the matter to consult a more generic manual of linguistics or diction.[66]

---

[64] Verdi - Cammarano, libretto of *Il Trovatore*, Act I.

[65] Verdi - Piave, libretto of *La Traviata*, Act II.

[66] For example, the manual by Corrado Veneziano quoted above.

This having been said, in Italian grammar the consonants are divided into:

- ✓ unvoiced: *c, f, p, q, t;*
- ✓ voiced: *b, d, g, l, m, n, r, v.*

This classification relates to the fact that, in being pronounced, these consonants provoke, or do not provoke, a vibration of the vocal cords and, although somewhat imprecise[67], it is useful to be familiar with it as a presupposition to some rules of pronunciation that we shall enumerate below.

- ✓ *n,* if it comes before *b* or *p*, becomes *m*: (*un bambino* → umbambino; *un palo* → umpalo; *in bici* → imbici; *nessun posto* → nessumposto);
- ✓ *s* is *unvoiced* → *s* if it comes at the beginning of the word (sabbia, sale) or of it precedes another *unvoiced consonant* (aspro, statua, esca);
- ✓ *s* is *voiced* → *z* if it precedes a *voiced consonant* (*sbaglio* → zbaglio; *slabbrato* → zlabbrato; *sgarrare* → zgarrare), or if it is intervocalic and placed in the middle of the word (*chiesa* → chiæza, *isola* → izola); composed lemmata consisting in a prefix plus a word beginning with *s* (such as *ri-sorsa, ri-sanare, a-sociale, de-saturato*) are not subject to this rule, for the *s* stays unvoiced as it would if it were the first letter of a word;
- ✓ *b* and *g,* if placed at the beginning of a word and are intervocalic, can well bear a slight emphasis, if thought necessary, in singing (una bbæella ggiornata), for this is typical of all Italian speech habits south of Tuscany;
- ✓ the groups *sc, gn, gl* are alternative orthographic representations of double consonants (but, in fact, almost *triple* in pronunciation, as seen above) *gn* → nnə; *gl* → llə; *sc* → sschə; they should therefore be emphasized and *very* energetically pronounced.

Finally, *z* can be *unvoiced* or *voiced*, but an overview is more complex than that of the *s*, since what in Italian is *orthographically synthesized* as "z" may, in effect, have various different origins:

---

[67] Technically all consonants can be uttered as if they were unvoiced, without involving the vocal cords.

- ✓ the *unvoiced z* → **ts** (often deriving from the – *ti+vowel* of classical Latin: *pretium*, Italian *prezzo* → pr<u>æ</u>ttso) is found:
    - when it is preceded by the letter *l* (*alzare* → alts<u>a</u>re):
    - when it is the initial letter of a word and the second syllable begins with an unvoiced consonants *c, f, p, q, t* (*zampa* → ts<u>a</u>mpa, *zufolo* → ts<u>u</u>folo);
    - if followed by an *i* which, in its turn, is followed by another vowel (*ozio* → <u>ao</u>tsio, *grazia* → gr<u>a</u>tsia);
    - in words ending in *-ezza, -ozza, -uzzo* (*finezza* → fin<u>e</u>ttsa, *merluzzo* → merl<u>u</u>ttso);
    - when infinitives end in *-azzare* (*starnazzare* → starnatts<u>a</u>re)
    - in the suffixes *-anza/-enza* (*speranza* → sper<u>a</u>ntsa, *credenza* → cred<u>æ</u>ntsa);
    - in the suffix *-onzolo* (*Raperonzolo* → Raper<u>o</u>ntsolo);
- ✓ the *voiced z* → **dz** (which often derives from *-di+vowel* in classical Latin: *prandium*, Italian *pranzo* → pr<u>a</u>ndzo) is, on the other hand, found:
    - in verbs with the suffix *-izzare* (*organizzare* → organiddz<u>a</u>re);
    - when it is an initial letter followed by two vowels (*zaino* → dz<u>a</u>ino, *zoo* → dz<u>ao</u>o);
    - when it is the initial letter of a word and the second syllable begins with one of the so-called voiced consonants *b, d, g, l, m, n, r, v* (*zebra* → dz<u>æ</u>bra);
    - when it is intervocalic (*azalea* → adzal<u>æ</u>a, *ozono* → odz<u>ao</u>no).

Syntactic germination (or doubling)

Without an adequate recognition and understanding of the *syntactic doublings* within the verse, it is not really possible to understand the phrasing that the composer has thought of for that phrase, and so one cannot either sing it or conduct it or play it appropriately. One must therefore be careful to thoroughly grasp the linguistic phenomenon that we are about to describe and analyze.

First of all, let it be clear that in a correctly spoken Italian: a consonant placed between two vowels, whether it is the initial letter of the word or in the middle of it (u**na**_**co**sa, a**mo**re_**m**io, la_**vi**ta) is to be pronounced as it is written: singular, level, simple, flowing – absolutely *not* doubled or stronger than normal, not even if we want to strengthen the meaning of the word in question (to this avail we shall make the best of the vowels we have, or possibly use the *schwa* as seen on page 56).

This *unless* that intervocalic consonant, but only when it is the *initial* of the word, is found in special, yet rather frequent cases that we shall illustrate shortly in detail: in such cases, the consonant will be doubled in speech: this is the typically Italian use of the *raddoppiamento fonosintattico* ("syntactic germination").[68]

Again:

> **syntactic germination occurs on the *initial* and *intervocalic* consonant of a word coming after specific types of words or situations.**

Doubling constitutes an essential characteristic of the language and is therefore obligatory in standard Italian diction, into which local speech habits intrude to varying degrees: increasingly towards the South and then decreasing, until finally disappearing, towards the North of Italy.[69]

It serves the fundamental purpose of rendering diction more intelligible, separating and defining acoustically the confines of the individual words in situations in which they could get lost, or in which confusion might arise (as,

---

[68] Warning: *doubling* must not be mistaken for the *double consonants*, those which are *identical twins and coupled when written* – and which, to be precise, must *always* be very exactly pronounced.

[69] The *raddoppiamento* is a rather unique prerogative of our language, not at all ignored but rather progressively more noticeable from Tuscany southwards (a Sicilian would go so far as to say *larrabbia*, doubling even the intervocalic *r*, as one would in Spanish) and less noticeable on the other hand as one travels northwards (the Venetians go so far as to completely omit the double consonants: *bello* becomes *bèo*; *capello, cavèo*).

for example, in phrases consisting of a succession of many monosyllables: "*se se ne va da qui*", "*chi fa per sé fa per tre*", etc.). But, even apart from its useful function in circumscribing words, it is obvious that the usefulness of doubling to the intelligibility of the Italian language is tied up with the *identification of the rhythm* for the ear that hears it,[70] given that the *accents* are the essence of the Italian language.

This doubling is somewhat a phenomenon of *physics*: it consists of the acoustic fusion of two different, adjoining consonants that, in order to avoid clashing in a cacophonic or clumsy *cluster*, blend into each other forming one single consonant, which as a result redoubles its energy.

The doubled consonant will always be the second in order of appearance from among the two, since the first, as we shall see, will never be represented in writing. For example, the preposition *a* has a more complete graphic form, which is *ad* (from the Latin *at*). We write *a casa*, but we read it as *acc**a**sa*, because between *a* and *casa* there lurks a phantom *d* that, although it has vanished from sight, remains very much alive in sound, but absorbed into the *c*, which comes out reinforced: *ad casa* → *acc**a**sa*. The full form *ad* will, on the other hand, be perfect for forming the *legato* before a word beginning with vowel (*ad_altra*), with the added advantage that it maintains the intelligibility and the distinction between the two lemmata (the form *a_altra* might unfortunately be taken for an attack of stuttering). The same thing occurs with the conjunctions *e* (from *ed*, Latin *et*) and *o* (from *od*, Lat. *aut*); we say *latte e miele* → *latte**mm**iæle* and *vero o falso* → *vero**ff**also* [71] in order to avoid the cacophony of *latte**d**miele*, *vero**d**falso*: the clash of consonants would be absolutely unbecoming to Italian vocalization, which rounds off all corners (even going so far as to pronounce the combination *gn* as /nnə/, whereas in any other language it preserves the guttural *g*).

For practice, let us therefore remember that:

---

[70] Marius Schneider, *Op. Cit.*: «In a desire to limit the extension of the *word* to its purely psychological aspect, one might say: the rhythm of the *word* emerges from common words, just as rage or goodness emerge from the stylistic melody of a phrase. While for us the word is reduced to being simply a denomination, the *word* is in truth the creative rhythm, it is the really true energetic substance through which the common word is permeated by a kind of magical intonation, through which different ordinary words can be penetrated by the same *word*.»

[71] See the rule on *crasis* on page 67.

> **1. doubling takes place after *a, e, o*;**
> that is, after the simple preposition *a* and after the conjunctions *e, o*.

And since Opera is full of interjections, let us also remember that:

> **2. doubling takes place after all *interjections*:**
> ***ah, eh, deh, oh, uh, ih, etc.***
> [Es. *ah sì* → ass<u>i</u>, *deh vieni* → dævvi<u>æ</u>ni; *oh Dio* → odd<u>io</u>].

Sometimes, in frequently used verbal associations, doubling goes so far as to change the spelling of the words, in order to assimilate them to speech, in the phenomenon known as *univerbation*: two lemmata that become united into one only (*da capo* → dacc<u>a</u>po). Some of the most common univerbations found in the Italian language will be useful for us here to understand and memorize some of the remaining cases that require doubling.

Univerbations such as *giammai, cosiddetto, laddove, neppure, siffatto, piuttosto* – that is, those composed of oxytone words (*già, così, là, né, sì, più*), remind us that:

> **3. doubling takes place after all *oxytone words***
> [e.g. *è mio* → <u>æ</u>mm<u>io</u>, *così bello* → cos<u>i</u>bb<u>æ</u>llo, *là sopra* → l<u>a</u>ss<u>o</u>pra; *perché no* → perch<u>e</u>nn<u>ao</u>].

Such univerbations as *daccapo, suddetto, frattanto, sebbene, chicchessia*, that is, words composed from various monosyllables (*da/su/fra/se/chi/che*), remind us that:

> **4. doubling generally takes place after *monosyllables***
> [e.g. *che fai* → cheff<u>ai</u>; *ma no* → mann<u>ao</u>; *chi sei* → chiss<u>æ</u>i; *se vai* → sevv<u>ai</u>].

Please note, though, that even if they are monosyllables we still do *not* double after:

- ✓ **all articles**: *lo, la, i, gli, le, una, uno;*
- ✓ **the preposition *di/de*** (presumably inherited from the Latin genitive, which was incorporated into the noun and implies belonging to the subject, but we cannot be sure of this);
- ✓ **the pronouns *mi/ti/gli/glie/si/se/ci/ce/vi/ve*,**

but paying attention to the fact that regular doubling takes place instead after *me, tu* and *te* (therefore we say *mi_piace* and *ti_dico*, but then we say *me solo* → messolo, *tu sei* → tussæi; we say *ti_va* but then we say *a te va* → attevva);

- ✓ **the particle *ne*** when without an accent.

These lastly mentioned cases are not followed by doubling for the reason that they have a too close syntactic relationship with the verb or noun they accompany to be acoustically separated from them. In fact, pronouns may even find themselves graphically *fused* to the verb, today just as yesterday: the *mi parla* of nineteenth century Opera has become *parlami;* viceversa, today's *ti vedo* will be found there as *veggoti;* Azucena's *mi vendica* is now vendicami; *ne andiam* became *andiamocene* as *vedraommi* became *mi vedrao,* etcetera. The same may be said for the article, indissolubly bound to its noun.

Univerbations such as *sopraffatto, Ognissanti*[72], *soprattutto*, remind us that:

> **5. doubling takes place after the words**
> ***come/dove/ogni/sopra/qualche***
> [e.g. *come sempre* → comessæmpre; *dove vai* → dovvevai; *ogni cosa* → ogniccaosa; *qualche modo* → qualchemmaodo].

With the constant aim of maintaining the intelligibility and the separateness of the words, we must remind the reader that, when reading or singing a

---

[72] "All Saints", the holiday that is celebrated in Italy on November 1st.

written text, in order to imitate what one would do to separate the various concepts in talking:

> **6. doubling takes place after all *punctuation marks***
> and therefore, by extension, after all ***musical pauses*** *
> [e.g. *pace, pace* → paceppa̲ce; *sì sì, no no* → si̲ssinnæonnæo;
> *deh, vieni, non tardar* → dehvviæninnontarda̲r].

Lastly:

> **7. the close encounter of the consonants *n* and *m*,
> results in a doubling of the *m***
> (and a complete elimination of the *n: un momento* → ummome̲nto;
> *in moto* → immao̲to].

Remember these two bits of advice when doubling consonants, where applicable;

1. In order to achieve a perfect doubling between two words, it is advisable to imagine adding the *extra* consonant not to the beginning of the *second* word (that whose initial consonant is being doubled), but at end of the *first* word, as if you were ideally compensating, making up for the truncation or elision that originated the doubling:

    a casa: not /a_cca̲sa/, but rather think /ac_ca̲sa/;

    è mio: not /è_mmio/, but rather think /èm_mi̲o/;

    e dai: not /e_ddai/, but rather think /ed_da̲i/;

    always making sure, though, that the doubling doesn't eat up the space and time of the preceding vowel, which must be kept intact in shape and length.

2. Whenever it is found difficult to effect the doubling of a consonant, our advice is to pull the ace from up your sleeve and refer to our friend *schwa*: skillfully employed. (Let us repeat this: the more *skillfully* we make use of it, the less will it be *noticeable*.) The *schwa*

helps us to preserve both *legato* and *doubling*, even if we steal a breath at the punctuation sign, especially if there is a musical pause coming up[73] (e.g.: *non so più* cosa son* cosa faccio* → nonsoppiu̯accosasonəccosafaccio; *Ah, tutto*, tutto*, finì* → Ahttutto*əttutto*əffini).

The consonant that it is desired to enhance will in this way stand out and be easier to manage *ad arte*.

Balance of the verse and equilibrium of the line

The reader will find here below a brief series out of a possibly *endless* number of examples of *balanced* verses (i.e. featuring an *acoustic equilibrium* within the line, or the lines of the strophe, or an aria) from operatic librettos: it might be useful to go through them in order to better understand the *radical* importance of precisely pronounced sung Italian for achieving good phrasing and complete comprehension of the score. These examples have been chosen almost at random from a comprehensive repertoire: the practice of balancing the verse, in which the *syntactic germination* (doubling) plays a crucial role, is in fact so much a fundamental part of versification that we meet with it *everywhere*, in *any* line of good poetry or kind of poetry in *any* historical period.

Let us then examine the following, renowned verses by highlighting how (and we will also briefly stop to consider *why*) they were phonetically balanced so well by the librettist, on the basic rules of diction we have learnt in the previous paragraphs of this book.

---

[73] From here on, breaths and musical pauses will be indicated by the sign "*".

Ex.1: Puccini, *Turandot*, Act III, *Nessun dorma*, Calaf:

	t-tt/d-dd/p-pp:	*in/æm/an/am/an:*
Tu pure o principessa, **Nella tua fredda stanza,** **Guardi le stelle,** **Che tremano d'amore** **E di speranza.** [74]	**tt**up**p**ureo**pp**rincipessa **nn**ella**t**ua**f**re**dd**as**t**anza **gg**ua**r**ə**d**illesə**t**elle **kk**e**tt**ræmano**dd**am**o**re e**dd**isəperanza	**tt**uppureopp**rin**cipessa **nn**ellatuafreddast**an**za **gg**uarədillesətelle **kk**e**ttræ**m**an**odd**am**ore e**dd**isəperanza
kk-gg:	*pur-pri-per/fr-rd-tr:*	*l:*
ttuppureopprincipessa nnellatuafr**e**ddastanza **gg**uarədillesət**e**lle **kk**ettræmanoddam**o**re eddisəperanza (mailmiomistæroæ**kk**i**u**zoimme...)	ttup**pur**eop**pri**ncipessa nnellatua**fr**edastanza **gg**ua**r**ədillesət**e**lle kke**tr**æmanoddam**o**re eddisə**per**anza	ttuppureopprincipessa nnel**l**atuafreddastanza ggua**r**ədi**l**lesəte**ll**e kkettræmanoddam**o**re eddisəperanza

The perfect interweaving of the many assonances conspires to achieve the idea of a *magic spell* (*cfr.* paragraph "Formula for ruling the movement of the stars" on page 136 of this book).

Ex. 2: Mozart, *Le nozze di Figaro*, Act III, *Dove sono i bei momenti*, Contessa.

Perché mai, se in pianti e in pene... [75]	**pp**erk**em**m**ai**s**eim**ə**pia**ntiei**m**ə**pe**ne

The *lamenting* of the broken-hearted wife is rendered through the alliteration of the *nasals* (*n, m*) and their vocalic associations *em/eim/en,* whereas the despair and sobbing are portrayed though the explosion of the consonant *p*; also note the assonance and symmetries in the groups of vowels *ai-ia/ei-iei,* depicting pain.

---

[74] "You too, O Princess, in your icy chamber, are looking at the stars, that tremble with love and hope."
[75] "How is it that if in bitter weeping…"

Ex. 3: Händel, *Giulio Cesare in Egitto*, Act III, *Piangerò la sorte mia*, Cleopatra.

Piangerò la sorte mia...[76]	piangerɔllasɔrtemia

In the metrically and phonetically illuminating libretto by Nicola Francesco Haym[77] it is very interesting and significant to see how, in a line of just four words, we find the perfect symmetry of rɔ/ɔr, with the doubled *ll* standing in the very middle of the verse as some sort of physical diaphragm between the two open tonic vowels and the two halves of the line; then comes the repetition of the painful *ia/ia* and finally the sighing effect of the *s* and of the soft *g*.

Ex. 4: Verdi, *Rigoletto*, Act I, *Pari siamo*, Rigoletto.

Io ho la lingua,	iɔllalingua
Egli ha il pugnale!	elləailpunnəale
Ma la saprò riprender!	mmallasaprɔrriprænder...
Ella è là...[78]	ellaælla...

The hatred and the disdain of the main character towards the Duke are expressed by: the percussive effect of *ɔl/al/ell/ail* (this assonance is echoed in the perfectly repetitive *ellaælla*), the strong *ng/gn/nn* groups and the raging *pr/rr*.

Ex. 5: Verdi, *La Traviata*, Act I, *È strano... Ah, fors'è lui... Sempre libera*, Violetta Valéry.

Che spero or più?	kkessəpærorəpiu
Che far degg'io?	kkeffarədeggio
Gioire![79]	ggioire

---

[76] "I shall weep over my fate..."
[77] Nicola Francesco Haym (1678 - 1729) was an Italian composer, cellist, librettist and impresario.
[78] "I have the tongue, he has the knife! But I know how to get her back! She is in there..."
[79] "What more can I hope for now? What should I do? Enjoy myself!"

Violetta passes from the sibilant desperation of the *k* and *s* (due to her tuberculosis) to the joyful leap of the *gg* in the perfect balance of *(cheffarde)****ggio/ggio****(ire)*.

Ex. 6: Gluck, *Orfeo*, Act III, Orfeo.

Ah, più non vive!	a**pp**i**u**nn**o**n**ə**v**i**ve
La chiamo invan!	llaki**a**moin**ə**v**an**
Saziati, sorte rea!	**ss**àziati, **ss**æ̀orteræa
Son disperato![80]	**ss**onədis**ə**per**a**to

Sadness, weeping and mourning are expressed in the *p* and in the *un /on /am/ in /an/ on*; despair and angry crying in the *iu/ia* and in the repeated *s/ss*.

Ex. 7: Rossini, *Il Barbiere di Siviglia*, excerpts from Acts I and II, Rosina.

Niente, niente, signore!	**nn**əænt**e**nnəæntess**i**nnə**o**re
Alla fin s'accheterà	allaf**i**nəs**akk**eter**a**
E contenta io resterò.	**e**kk**o**ntæntaiorester**æ**
Mi lascio reggere,	**mm**ilaxoræ**gg**ere
Mi fo guidar.	**mm**if**æ**o**gg**uid**a**r
Di sorpresa e di contento	**dd**isorpr**e**za***edd**icontænto
Son vicina a delirar!	**ss**onəvic**i**na*a**dd**elir**a**r
Ah, tu solo, amor, tu sei...[81]	a**ttuss**oloam**o**rə**ttuss**æi...

---

[80] "Ah, she lives no longer! It is useless my calling to her! Evil destiny, are you glutted now? I am in despair!"

[81] "Nothing at all, Sir! [...] In the end he will calm down and I shall be satisfied. [...] I let them rule me, I let them guide me. [...] With surprise and delight, I am near to losing my head. [...] Ah, love, you alone can..."

It is interesting to note how the initial *n* of *niente, niente,* twice doubled, spontaneously becomes in pronunciation indistinguishable from the *gn* of *signore*. Then notice the symmetric *akke/ekko*, and the matching of the soft *gg* of *reggere* with the hard *gg* of *guidar*. Later on the explosion of the *d* signifies the character's surprise in discovering the true identity of her lover and the reiteration of the *tt-ss* seems to mimic the beating of a loving heart.

Now the reader can amuse himself by doing the same type of analysis: looking at literally *any* line in *any* Opera libretto that he knows or that he is studying, but it might as well be the first he lights upon, amuse himself by examining, observing carefully *all* the syntactic doublings present in it, stopping to consider the consonantal balancing techniques, the assonances, the symmetries and the alliterations, with a view to pronouncing it correctly, and so bringing out its structure, which is the *scaffolding* of the musical phrasing.

Check!

Let us reinforce the clarity of what has been so far explained and check the effective amount learned by doing the following exercise, properly filling in, in the text of the famous Mozartean *canzone* proposed here below, all the empty spaces (_). Use a dictionary, as advised at the beginning[82], to verify the orthoepy of the vowels.

N.B. The student must breathe *only* at the sign (*), without ever breaking the line elsewhere: he *must* accustom himself to foreseeing the whole shape and length of the phrase *before* singing it, to instinctively calculate in his *inspiration* (literal and metaphorical) the type of energy and the right amount of breath to sustain every phrase to its very end; in fact, he must *make use* of any lack of breath for purposes of expression, training himself not to give way to panic (as panic leads to consuming even *more* oxygen) and apply himself with all his being to the vivacity of his mental diction to make up for any difficulties, cunningly transforming them into *interpretation* and *emotion* (in real life, we often speak *breathlessly* when feeling emotional).

Voi, che sapete	__ oi__e__ap_e_te
Che cosa è amor,	kkekk_zaææam_r*
Donne, vedete	dd_nne__ed_e_te
S'io l'ho nel cor.	s_i_olæo __elǝc_r*
Quello ch'io provo	__uellokiopr_vo
Vi ridirò;	viridiræo*
È per me nuovo,	æ __erǝmennu_vo*
Capir nol so.	__ap_i_r_nnolǝs_*
Sento un affetto	ss_ntounaff_tto
Pien di desir	pi_nǝdidez_i_r*
Ch'ora è diletto,	kk_raæ __ilætto*
Ch'ora è martir.	kk_raæ __ar_t_i_r*
Gelo e poi sento	__ æloepp_is_nto
L'alma avvampar,	lal_mavvamp_a_r*

---

[82] We again recommend the *Treccani* dictionary, also available online.

E in un momento *Torno a gelar.*	einu__omento t_rnoa__elar*
Ricerco un bene *Fuori di me,* *Non so chi 'l tiene,* *Non so cos'è.*	__ic_rcou_b_ne ffu_ridime* __onəsɑo __ilti_ne* __onəsɑo __osæ*
Sospiro e gemo *Senza voler;* *Palpito e tremo* *Senza saper,*	__ospiroegg_mo* ssæntsavoler* __alpitoettr_mo* ss_ntsasap_r*
Non trovo pace *Notte né dì:* *Ma pur mi piace* *Languir così.*	__onətr_vopace nn_tteneddi* __a__urəmipiace lanəguirəcozi...

(The reader will find the correct solution in the note below[83], for it is a very difficult exercise to demand from a beginner, such as we suppose the reader to be.)

The singer should now amuse himself by copying on the left-hand side an aria chosen at will from his repertoire – taking care to get hold of its correct text from a good edition of the libretto – and to continue by doing, on the right-hand side, the same task that he applied to the Mozart aria above. In this, as in every other art, to copy (especially *by hand*) is effectively half of the way toward learning deeply.

---

[83] Vvoikkessapete ssæntounaffætto rricercoumbæne nnonətrɑovopace
kekkɑozaæamor* piænədidezir* ffuɑoridime* nnɑotteneddi*
ddɑonnevvedete kkoraæddilætto* nnonəsɑokkiltiæne* mmappurəmipiace
siolɑonneləcɑor* kkoraæmmarətir* nnonəsɑokkosæ* llanəguirəcozi...

qquellokioprɑovo ggæloeppɑoisænto ssospiroeggæmo*
viridirɑo* laləmavvampar* ssæntsavoler*
æpperəmennuɑovo* einummomento ppalpitoettræmo*
kkapirənnoləsɑo* tornoaggelar* ssæntsasaper*

Singing Neapolitan

It is often forgotten that Neapolitan is not a dialect, but a language complete in itself, with a very strict and complex grammar, and iron rules of pronunciation which mostly singers do not bother to master before launching into the highly prized repertory of classic Neapolitan songs.

Remember that, in Neapolitan:

- ✓ as is the case in all southern Italian speech,[84] for the general Italian principle mentioned above, all the atonal *e* and *o* vowels and all the atonal final vowels turn into *schwa* /ə/ (e.g. *bellezza* → bəll<u>e</u>zzə; *stenditoio* → stənnət<u>u</u>rə);
- ✓ the intervocalic *d* sometimes becomes *r* [85] (e.g.: *Madonna* → Mar<u>o</u>nnə) even at the beginning of a word, if there is no doubling (e.g.: *che stai dicendo* → chə st<u>a</u>yə risc<u>æ</u>nnə);
- ✓ The *s* coming before another consonant, if this is *unvoiced*, is pronounced like the Italian /schə/ (*sposa* → schəp<u>o</u>sə), but if this is voiced the *s* is said as in the French "*je*"(e.g.: *sbagliato* → jbagli<u>a</u>tə);
- ✓ the *gl* group is pronounced like the *y* of *yogurt*, but doubled (e.g. *figli* → f<u>i</u>yyə);
- ✓ the *gua* is pronounced like the English *w* (that is, a *double-u*, as in *what*; e.g. *guaglione* → wayy<u>o</u>nə).

To offer a little practice, we here present the text of the above-mentioned masterpiece, with orthoepic transcription:

Che bella cosa, na jurnata 'e sole;	kkəbb<u>æ</u>llac<u>ao</u>sənnayurənat<u>e</u>sol<u>ə</u>*
N'aria serena, dopo na tempesta!	nn<u>a</u>ryasər<u>e</u>nadd<u>ao</u>ppənatəmp<u>æ</u>sta*
Pe' ll'aria fresca pare già na festa.	ppəll<u>a</u>ryafreschkaparəgi<u>a</u>nnaf<u>æ</u>sta*
Che bella cosa, na jurnata 'e sole!	kkəbb<u>æ</u>llac<u>ao</u>sənnayurənat<u>e</u>sol<u>ə</u>*

---

[84] Roberto Caprara, *Dizionario etimologico e grammatica del dialetto parlato a Massafra*, Antonio Dellisanti Editore, 2014.

[85] Note by Michael Aspinall: singers should note that this transformation of the intervocalic *d* in *r* is not to be found in recordings of Neapolitan songs made before 1940.

Ma n'atu sole	mmannatusolə*
Chiu' bello, oi ne'	cchiubbælloinæ*
'O sole mio	osolǝmiǝ*
Sta 'nfronte a te!	stanəfrontatte*
Lucene 'e lastre d'a fenesta toia;	llucənellastrərafənæstatoyə*
Na lavannara canta e se ne vanta.	nnalavannaracantaessənəvanta*
E pe' tramente torce, spanne e canta.	eppətramæntətaorcəschəpanneccantə*
Lucene 'e lastre d'a fenesta toia.	llucənellastrərafənæstatoyə*
Ma n'atu sole...	mmannatusolə*...
Quanno fa notte e 'o sole se ne scenne	qquannəfanaotteosoləsənəscennə*
Me vene quase 'na malincunia	mməvænəquasənamalincunia*
Sotto 'a fenesta toia restarria	ssottafənæstatoyarəstarria*
Quanno fa notte e 'o sole se ne scenne	quannəfanaotteosoləsənəscennə*
Ma n'atu sole...	mmannatusolə*...

V. Errors

"The German, Russian and Italian languages have all deteriorated in the last ten or fifteen years as a result of dictatorship. But if thought corrupts language, language can also corrupt thought. A bad usage can spread by tradition and imitation, even among people who should and do know better."

George Orwell,
Politics and the English Language

Impostures and impostors

Any day when a singing teacher asks his unfortunate pupil to make "*a sound that is more beautiful/rounded/supported/brilliant*" without telling him that this result could only be achieved through an adequate conception of the *vowel* that informs it, that stretches beneath it, that is implicit within it since its conception; or, even worse, whenever that teacher asks his pupil to sacrifice that vowel to the illusion of sound, to mask it a little in order to imitate the mature sound of the experienced artist – there you are. That is how we say farewell to the art of Belcanto to sadly welcome an era of *musical narcissism*, i.e. of an attitude to singing in which the acoustic *image* prevails over the substantial *matter*, progressively making it null and forgotten in its powers and reason of being. Given that we have been living for decades in the era of records[86], consequently singers tend to imitate them with an acoustic *cut-and-paste* method, a situation exacerbated by internet; yet internet could be a good instrument for singers. This treaty was written with the main purpose of showing readers how to rediscover truth and meaning where passive listening and sometimes nonsensical imitation has settled in, at the expense of a truly artistic experience.

The teacher who advises his pupil to set about *forging water* (which we use as a metaphor just because it is something elusive, yet not so elusive as

---

[86] Plato, in his *Phaedrus*, in the same way makes Thamus, king of Thebes, ciaim to have invented writing, rather than its real inventor, the God Theuth: *"You give your disciples the appearance of knowledge, but not the real thing: through you they hear many things without real teaching, and will think they know many things, whilst on the whole they are ignorant of them, and they will be bad company, because they have become carriers of opinions rather than wise men."*

sound!) instead of, more sensibly, trying to forge what contains it (the wineskin that preserves it, the well that gathers it, the tubes that transmit it) is guilty of an illogical *imposture* and contributes to filling the Opera market with professional *water forgers;* impostors, mostly unaware of being so, though highly paid. These are people who have forgotten that to be able to carry this water around to irrigate and to quench thirst, something is necessary to contain it, and that the quality of the container will determine either the good use or the waste of the water, the possibility of transporting it far off or not, its range, its good health, and even its taste.

As long as the pupil is called upon to make "an *a* more like an *o*" or "an *i* inclining towards a French *u*", he will be trapped in a lie, an *imposture* that, being such, will instill in him insecurity and a progressive *impostor syndrome*: he will be condemned to restricted thinking and this will prevent him from launching the phrase, the character, the rôle; he will be denied access to the sacred, dramatic and thespian *inspiration,* which is an essential and integral part of vocal technique. Let us repeat this concept:

> ***interpretative diction*** **is part of the vocal technique required to perform a piece,**

an essential and indispensable part, and it does not involve any mental modification within the body of the word, which stays untouched, as the ultimate mental anchor to cling on to.

It would be more pertinent to ask the pupil to sing precisely *that* vowel (abstract entity from our left hemisphere, as all language is, untouched and untouchable), but sing it in *that* particular way, suggesting *that* emotion suitable to *that* discourse of *that* character just as *that* composer meant it for *that* moment of *that* piece! There are only seven abstract Italian vowels – yes – and they are to be kept the same, *mentally*, at all times – yes – but they will be interpreted through endless different nuances, colors and vocal attitudes! This will intuitively make the execution of any passage or phrase much easier, since a composer never conceives the phrasing of a vocal line leaving out the interpretative component, which is its *interpretative diction*. As we approach the modern age it will be more and more explicitly asked for in the scores: *con dolore, con rabbia, ridendo, dolcissimo...* Requesting *interpretative diction* from the student is quite the opposite of asking him to think and sing "omore" instead of *amore,* or "trana" instead of *trono*. The *linguistic thought*, the abstract conception of the word and vowel, not only has *always* to stay true to itself and *always* uncontaminated by any sounds in the singer's mind, but its incorrupted purity will in fact be the very warranty of the good health of every sound, of good carriage and *squillo* even on the lowest notes, of organic homogeneity in the *passaggi di registro* ("changes of register", especially when the voice must cover wide, abrupt intervals). All in all, such incorrupted linguistic thinking will keep *a real thread of thought* in the singer's mind, that will help him to *mean* whatever he is singing, to interpret it, and therefore to sing it well; instead of just making pompous, supposedly "beautiful" sounds that will make everything he sings the same, soon turning his performance into something predictable and boring.

How many teachers send their own pupils around with their voices in ruins, to sing arias that seem taped together, as if they were a Harlequin's costume, all with unequal *patches* of voice and vowels, each one adapted to the demands of the pitch, to *that* single note! Where will these singers rediscover that unified, coherent, elegant design in the discourse and therefore in the vocal line, that is no other than a *vocalic* line that determines the phrasing?

The nearer we go back in time to the origins of Opera, so much less in number do we find – notice this – the words contained in an aria: very few, chosen with taste and placed by the author with the same maniacal care that a professional *parfumeur* would bestow upon choosing the essences for the perfume of a prestigious *maison;* just a few, then repeated *ad infinitum*. Those words were repeated, yes: to enchant the ears of the listeners, but also for the joy of the great singers of the day, for whom those few words with their vowels were a solid canvas on which they could rival one another in whirlwind improvisations, having them as a solid structure they could cling to. The *vowel*: the rope-walker's rope, the acrobat's trapeze, the safety net for the woman shot from a cannon. If the singer is clear as to what vocalic volume he is moving through or which one is coming up, his musical mind – in the other hemisphere, over there – will be free to glide and to take flights with guaranteed success; free to follow the impetus of the melody as if extemporizing, thanks to the security offered by vocalic rigour – if respected.

Today the vowels – the supporting structures – are missing. And, incidentally, we do not *create* any more when singing: we mostly *cut-and-*

paste from what is in our acoustic memory of the recordings we have heard (even our own recordings) – and that is all. Where the external appearance of sound reigns, there is no place for improvisation and creativity. It will happen that in the same aria the words *amore* and *onore*, though repeated incessantly, will be pronounced – through the power of an almost perverse force – in a different way each time: for, depending on where and how those words are set, the singer will distort and violate them however he pleases, adapting their sacred prosody to his own inefficiency. Here an open vowel, there – the same vowel of the same word – closed; here a word with a consonant arbitrarily doubled, there the same consonant completely omitted... All this conspires to remove that minimum of *acoustic symmetry* understood even by newborn babies – to whom, not by chance, we sing nursery rhymes – *the rhyme*, indeed! That which even a few months-old child can understand is lacking from the Opera market today. (It is also lacking among singers and teachers who are – *ahimè* – Italian.)

Chewed legato, *wet* speech

It is typical of those many singers whose vocal technique involves muscular effort, due to technical ineptitude or simply to their native language, to make audible, because of its slowness, the process of opening the wide vowels and closing the narrow, or the passing from one to the other. Quite simply: it is essential for the singer to avoid any kind of vowel emission *in fieri*, that is, in which the process of opening or closing the vowel, of shaping it, can be heard (*amorey miow, suordo orechiow, bwella dwonna*) – since Italian vowels are *stable* and reach the listening ear already "perfectly formed"; this is essential so that the *legato* may remain *linear* and not assume a wave-like motion. The secret will lie in teaching the pupil, here too, to think of the vowels sufficiently ahead of time in the mind and at the same time to relax all the apparatus of the mouth – and in particular the lips and the tongue – in such a way as to make it *inactive* and so more quickly receptive to the dictates of this mental anticipation of the vocal act. To repeat:

> the abstract quality and the perfection of the vocal volumes of Italian in themselves guarantee a good legato, which can only be obtained thanks to the total independence of diction (abstract) from phonation (physical).

(Lastly, and this is particularly directed at readers of the Saxon group: now and always take care to *dry* all your consonants in the Italian sunshine, in particular the *t* and the *d*: place the tip of your tongue *between* the two rows of teeth: not higher up, on the hard palate, and thus suddenly exploding these consonants by suddenly releasing the tongue in pronouncing: t**u**t**to**, a**d**a**tt**o, s**o**t**to**, t**æs**t**a**).

When the *letter* becomes threatening

And the teacher wrote the alphabet for him and began to practice it many times, but the child [Jesus] said nothing and did not answer him for a long time. Becoming outraged, the teacher hit him on the head. After enduring this stoically, the child said to him, "I am teaching you more than being taught by you because I know the letters you are teaching me and your judgment is great. These things are to you like a copper pitcher or a clashing cymbal which do not offer glory or wisdom through sound. Nobody understands the power of my wisdom." Then, when his rage was finished, he said the alphabet from alpha to omega very quickly. Looking the teacher in the face, he told him, "Since you do not know the nature of the alpha, how are going to teach me the beta? Hypocrite, if you know, first teach me the alpha then I will believe what you say about the beta." Then, he began to tell the teacher about the first letter. And the teacher was not strong enough to say anything. Then, while many were listening, he said to Zacchaeus, "Listen, teacher, and observe the structure of the first letter, how it has two standard lines and impresses coming to a point in the middle and remaining there, coming together, lifting up, dancing, having three corners, having two corners, without strokes, of one family, well-balanced, as long as the alpha has equal lines."

Apocriphal Gospels - Infancy Gospel of Thomas

The reader will know those anonymous, threatening letters in old detective films, made from different-sized letters cut out from newspapers and then glued together to form a complete sentence, intelligible but very unpleasant; the mere thought of them brings on anxiety. Well: many performances, vocal and *vocalic*, are the precise homology of those letters, and in fact they produce the same upsetting, unbalancing effect.

As a matter of fact, our ear delights in *symmetry*, in *repetition*, in *patterns*: basically, it is the satisfaction of a created expectancy, the resolution of a tension, the reply to a question, that which the world calls *beauty*.

Italian operatic singing cannot do without a *design* founded on a mastery of the sound of its basic *raw material*, we cannot go on singing by means of patching: *phrasing* is essential, we must always be *stylists* of our own musical discourse, and *trust* that the right *mental design* of the vowel will give place to the physical response necessary to obtain it. Let us repeat this concept another three times, just to be sure, because it is one of the fundamental ideas that this book wishes to convey and the reason why it has been written.

> We need to ***trust*** that the correct picturing of the vowel will *automatically* give rise to the physical response necessary to obtain it.
>
> **We need to *trust* that the correct picturing of the vowel will *automatically* give rise to the physical response necessary to obtain it.**
>
> **WE NEED TO <u>*TRUST*</u> THAT THE CORRECT PICTURING OF THE VOWEL WILL <u>*AUTOMATICALLY*</u> GIVE RISE TO THE PHYSICAL RESPONSE NECESSARY TO OBTAIN IT.**

At that point, and only at that point, just as the artesian well will gather the rainwater to itself when it falls, and the water will know how to flow into it without any effort, as lightning will find the way to the lightning conductor installed there on purpose, as the skillfully designed architecture of a building will filter the light of sunset exactly as the architect had imagined, as the nest prepared on the veranda will attract the swallows: this is how the vowel will *materialize* the voice.

It will be all in vain to try *a posteriori* to circumscribe a shapeless *blob* of sound, after it has been uttered, hoping to disguise it as a vowel: *in the beginning* – was the Word.

It is important that all the equal vowels are always identical every time: each closed *e* must be judged to be identical, with exactly the same character (they will only be invigorated and coloured by emotive diction, but their abstract *mental orthoepia* will remain faithful to itself everywhere) and the same is true for all the other vowels: they do not change their *font* according to the singer's whim or their position on the bar lines. As they are abstract volumes, and as they are only seven in number, the singer must be sure to keep them identical, true to themselves, always and everywhere: he will be enormously helped and reassured in his emission by this constancy and identity, and the ear of the audience will perceive an *order,* a *pattern,* a *spell* – an *enchantment* – by which it will be deeply satisfied and thrilled.

What about the *æ?*

In singing too, all the vowels have the right to live.

Tullio Serafin

They seem to have gone out of fashion in the world of Opera. The palette of Italian has only seven colours and we have lost one of them along the way. For "*the sound is backward*", for "*the sound is squashed*", for "*the sound is white*": the truth is, those who say such things lack a clear mental image of this lovely vowel; they do not understand its nature nor its essence, they consider it an obstacle rather than a means of expression, even *if* they do identify it as a vowel in its own right and that they are able at least to discern its exact acoustic profile.

And yet, the *æ* has all the ineffable poetry of a blossoming flower, *while* it is blooming. The poetry of everything that is opening or will not resign itself to closing, that filters light in the *tætro* ("gloomy") and in the *tænebre* ("darkness"), giving *solliævo* ("relief") in trouble. It is the warmth of *bæne* ("love") and the light of *spæme* ("hope"); the misty melancholy of the *mæsto* ("sad"), the frenetic anxiety of the *præsto*.

The acoustic flattening resulting from changing all the *æ* vowels into its closed homologue *e* – as we can hear today done routinely by singers who often are unaware of what they do and of the damage that they are doing (also to themselves) – is dreadful, if we consider that in Italian the open vowels are already a spare minority and that a librettist knew very well what he was doing, placing them strategically to create a spot of light. (Incredibly, the most common mistake made by whoever is learning to speak Italian is to open all the vowels…. except for those very *æ* in singing!)

For this reason, we repeat, in this present manual we have clearly made the *æ* derive from the written *a*, writing it in its classical Latin form: because it must preserve all the physical amplitude of the *a*, its facial imperturbability, its blessed repose, its depth, its roundness. It will be the brain, giving imperceptible direction to the tongue that the singer must neither think about nor even be aware of, that will give us that particular variation of vocalic aperture of such changing, luminous, rarified colour, which pertains especially to *æstasi* ("ecstasy").

The author here launches a desperate appeal: let us restore the *æ*. Thank you.

Arbitrary doubling

The ten years of Italian diction coaching that the author has drawn upon to write this manual have inspired the following *Murphy's law* of doubling:

- ✓ *Axiom* of arbitrary doubling: «The singer whose mother tongue is not Italian and who, even though he is not familiar with the rules of doubling, will want to mimic the musicality of the language in singing, will execute doubling just the same, through random imitation and *regularly in the wrong place*.»
    - o First *corollary*: «For motives still not cleared up, the singer will double a consonant even more insistently when it should really be pronounced smoothly.»
    - o Second *corollary*: «Even that singer whose mother tongue is Italian, together with all others, will keep on arbitrarily doubling consonants, parroting the mistakes he has heard in historical recordings by great foreign singers, whom he tends to imitate, with no spirit of criticism (or patriotic pride).»

How to remedy all this?

- ✓ First *observation*: «The singer will not succeed in eliminating the defect in diction mentioned in the first corollary, except by *completely eliminating the consonant erroneously doubled,* as an exercise».

The singer is advised, furthermore, not to reinsert that consonant until he has repeated the phrase over and over again, eliminating it – that is, before he has memorized the correct verbal prosody of the text. For example, *sempre libera* should be pronounced without doublings; however the soprano, through imitating others, will systematically go on singing *semprellibera*: therefore, eliminate the *l* completely, repeating *sempre_ibera* – following Verdi's *staccato* marking – until the mistaken reflex of the tongue has been eradicated; remember that the consonant that must not be doubled may in some cases be eliminated even definitively – that is, even onstage, in performance – without compromising the intelligibility of the word: The hearing of the audience, which is neither literary nor diachronic and is essentially *rhythmic* (rather as in the case of animals, see note 70), will however hear *sempre libera*.

- ✓ Second observation: «In the learning phase, the singer will only succeed in slackening the tension of the false doubling by sloughing it off *elsewhere.*»

So you are advised above all to make sure of the correct intensity of enunciation of the orthographic doublings and of the syntactic germinations necessary to the prosody, even going so far as to create a few *unnecessary* ones, so long as they are in "innocuous" places – with the intention of re-establishing an acoustic balance to the inexpert singer's ear, until he learns to do without superfluous doublings.

This tip is extremely helpful in the very frequent case of articles followed by words starting with consonants (*la sorte mia, la paterna mano*, etc.), as well as for the preposition *di* and for all other cases listed on page 67 as exceptions to the fourth rule of doubling (see page 73).

Example: instead of "*vvengalammæorte*" – wrong, rhetorical and ugly – sing and let it be sung rather as "*vvæengallamæorte*": because in the case in question the dramatic stress of the word under consideration should be given to the vowel, leaving space for it, and to the group of consonants in the middle of the word." In fact, when a word does not call for a mandatory doubling on its *initial* consonant, its consonants to be stressed in the diction will usually be the middle ones that are the closest ones to the tonic vowel (usually the ones immediately following it, but sometimes the ones preceding it), given that they are doubles or groups of consonants (in this latter case the use of the *schwa* will be precious:

la rabbia → llar**a**__**bb**__ia, *di colpo* → ddic**o**__**lə**__p__o__, *la vivrò* → llav__i__**vər**__ə__).

By exalting *the intermediate consonants* in the word, it will be immediately evident how they will go on to balance – through assonances, alliterations and symmetries – the other nearby consonants in the context of the verse: a sign that the librettist had foreseen the phenomenon and acted accordingly (see the paragraph on the balance of the verse on page 76).

Syllabication

Let it be remembered, in musical examples indicating *staccato* or with words whose syllables are even interspersed with pauses (to represent laughter, weeping, surprise, anxiety), that the subdivision of the *sound* of the word will not be done according to the *grammatical* rules of *subdivision into syllables*, since that would seem unnatural and not very convincing: the syllables, however *implied*, that is finishing in consonants in their grammatical division (see note 48), that we marked in bold in the following chart, will be interrupted after their last vowel and their final consonant will be sent on to begin the following syllable.

Original Text	Grammatical Syllabication	To Be Sung
Fredda ed immobile	Fred-da ed im-mo-bi-le	Fre*ddae-di-mm__ə__*bile
Ah, fors'è lui	Ah, for-s'è-lu-i	Ah*ffo*(r)s'è*llu̲i;
Ah, infelice cor tradito, per angoscia non scoppiar	Ah, in-fe-li-ce cor tra-di-to per an-go-scia non scop-piar	Ah__i__(*n)feli*cec__ə__(*r)tradi*to pe(*r)ang__ə__*sciano(*n) scoppia̲r

In the last example the consonant that make the grammatical syllable "implicate" or "closed" (that is, the consonant that ends it: again, see note 48) has been placed in brackets because it is always possible to leave it out, or rather, it will always be possible to replace it with the emotional sigh (due to anxiety, joy, surprise, laughter, sobbing, whatever) that originally inspired the composer to write a *staccato*: not only will the audience not notice the omission, but they will even follow the text better.

VI. How to study

The singer, having pulled himself together and being happily in the mood for singing, concentrates on always mentally preparing what he is about to sing and this is that famous foresight that prepares him for execution, making it easier for him and more lovely, welcome and inspiriting for the listener.

Giambattista Mancini,
Pensieri e Riflessioni Pratiche sopra il Canto Figurato

Step 1: Text

We have already seen – but it is as well to say it again, again and again – that text and music appertain to two distinct and *physically separated* hemispheres of the human brain, so it will be as well to make them work separately until each of them has mastered his business.

Therefore, when studying a new piece, or in restudying one you already know, it will be as well to keep in mind this physiological separation: it is better not to mix the study of the words with that of the music, giving absolute priority to the former, so as to run precisely through the creative process of the composer. We shall, therefore, do exactly what Verdi did: reciting the lines that his librettists provided (after endless bargaining) until they spontaneously established themselves in a melodic space, which the composer – as he himself says in his letters– only had to set down on paper.[87]

It is an excellent exercise (absolutely *indispensable* for the foreign singer) to write down the words of the piece being studied[88] – *by hand* – on one page; on this the orthoepic notes should be inserted, having been previously looked up and verified.

The next step is to read the text aloud, with its correct orthoepy and prosody: one, ten, twenty, a hundred times, until it runs perfectly smoothly and every

---

[87] «Yesterday, after having replied to your letter, I set myself to study the fourth act duet for a long time, and I am ever more convinced that, right from the beginning, it must be given a lyrical shape. I even got mixed up with the heptasyllables in the words of the recitative, and I saw that a melody could be made here.»; Verdi, letter to the librettist of *Aida* Antonio Ghislanzoni, 1870.

[88] As in the checking example, page 82.

detail and sound ravine has been mastered (you will be surprised at how many details will pop up at each reading).

Only then will the student go on to completely study the residual meaning of words (that is, the part that he has not picked up already through the sound), translating it into his own mother tongue – first word for word and then in a more general and at the same time personal and introspective sense (see the sample on page 154) – but he will do this *on a separate piece of paper.* [89]

> Please note that each of the two pieces of paper *must be strictly monolingual*, and the singer must work on each one *separately*.

The singer, in fact, does not need to be able to translate one text into another, for he is an interpreter and not a translator; he needs instead to memorize each version *separately*, and with different aims. He will use the original Italian text to think aloud in a language more or less strange to him, made up on the whole of concrete sounds and abstract vowels, and he will absorb the character portrayed in a certain manner (through phonemes, syllables, doublings, colours, onomatopoeias).

With the text translated into his own mother tongue, on the other hand, the mental process will be different and the shades of meaning grasped will also be different: precedence will be given to the *narrative* and *psychological aspects*, intrapersonal, which will greatly help the singer to dig deep into the original in Italian (also – but not only – for what concerns the mnemonic aspect).

(In the appendix to this book, from page 153 on, the reader will find a sample of such a study, plus some space reserved for him to do this type of exercise on his own repertoire, and so solidify and verify what has just been

---

[89] It is rather like studying a new language: the worst way of learning it is to translate it into your own (or, worse still, translate your own into the foreign one), because that implies that your brain performs two efforts at the same time, furthermore, each very different from the other; in order to assimilate new structures quickly without confusing them with the old ones you must work in one language at a time, thinking directly in the new language (translation requires quite another type of mental work, superfluous and even harmful in itself to the learning of the language).

prescribed, and in this way preserve, together with the book, a personal contribution to this study that will help him to grasp this technique.)

Step 2: Psalmody (rhythm + dynamics)

Once the text has been learned in all its aspects: rhythm, sound and meaning – separately – the second step, of fundamental importance to the singer in the process of *getting his voice round the piece*, will be to chant it as a *psalmody*,[90] that is, all on the one same note, chosen in the medium-low speaking register and in a more or less supported *mezza voce*, but using the composer's rhythm – *precisely*.

This work may be done, if you like, with the musical score in front of you, but at first declaiming the text in its precise *rhythm*: that is, keeping the melody *out* of it. Or, you may transcribe the text for yourself on a stave of music, writing only the time signal and the stems (without the round notes), so that you can be sure of not being tempted to sing something that you have not yet entirely mastered phonetically and muscularly.

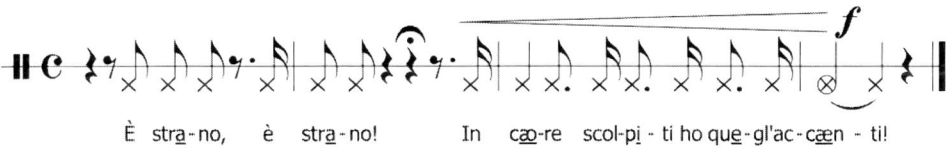

È stra-no, è stra-no!   In cao-re scol-pi - ti ho que-gl'ac-cæn - ti!

Fig. 5. Giuseppe Verdi, *La Traviata,* **Finale Act One.**
The *legatura* ("slur") over *accenti* is here meant to indicate *portamento;* instead the pupil may draw a double slur, or one of a different colour, to indicate a *tie*, amusing himself by creating his own personalized textual scores, which will help him a lot in his studies.

In this way the singer will get used to forming the required vowels, *a tempo*, but always thinking and designing them ahead, without ever distorting them in the effort of adapting them to a certain note, thanks to the strategic choice of chanting a *monotone,* some sort of *litany* which may then be lightly and

---

[90] *Salmo*, from the Greek, *psalmòs*, means "leap". And the *leap* is, in its nature, a rhythmical gesture.

progressively varied so as to increasingly approach the melody written by the composer.

By adhering to this method, the singer *will memorize muscularly the correct vocalic volumes* (which, as ascertained right from the first chapter, do not vary with the varying intonation) together with psycho-physical sensations of mastery, comfort and control, which – when they have become automatic – will never leave him when the melody and its intervals come into play.

To develop a happily comfortable muscular memory means to have done more than half the work. Developing an unhappily uncomfortable one is, on the other hand, a death sentence, that sometimes one can carry around for a lifetime and that can alienate a piece or even a career to the point of renunciation. What a pity: something that could so easily have been prevented, or cured, with this hygiene of learning.

Step 3: Melody

Once the text has been assimilated with all its predetermined *time* and *rhythm*, we must consider what *tone* the composer has given it. At first, it is better to play the vocal line on a keyboard without even chanting it: in this phase the singer will concentrate on the markings indicating dynamics, breaths and pauses, committing them to memory without singing anything. Then we will be able to play the well—mastered melody on our instrument while at the same time chanting in a monotone the previously memorized text in its given rhythm.

Never sing the melody of the piece during the first days of this study (the risk is that of acquiring a muscular memory of the mistakes and the muscular tensions of our first attempts at something we don't yet completely possess).

In other words, we do *not* sing, until we possess, perfectly but *separately*, the memory of each component: the *textual-rhythmical* and the *melodic*.

Consequently:

we sing by heart or we never sing at all.

Restrict yourself to repeating the operations described above until, at a certain point, the piece will begin to sing itself, in such a way as to be difficult to hold back and without any physical effort being necessary.

Learning to *think*: two rules

> First rule: while singing, one does *not* think and simultaneously emit the sound.

Please note that this is not a piece of advice, but simply a matter of the real facts of the case: the two actions – thinking and emitting sound – *are* in fact out of phase, with a time lag that at times amounts to almost a second and which can be as much longer as we are expert. Never forget this principle nor ever wander away from it, because all our motory actions are based on it:

> **the brain instructs <u>BEFORE</u> the body executes.**

This is true even when there is an appearance of perfect synchronism.[91] (On condition that the brain instructs *tout court;* that is, on condition that the singer be aware that the work of mental instruction is his responsibility, that it depends on his brain and his concentration, and let him not imagine that he can sing just like that, by pure luck.)

A tennis player – to give an example – does not decide what arm movement to make when the ball, shot at him by his adversary at 250 kilometres per hour, has already hit its mark. A tennis player gets his stroke ready even before hearing the smack of his adversary's, because from hearing that smack he will have scarcely a *third* of a second before he has to hit back. He gets ready for it by observing his adversary moving and so automatically instructs his arm, which *reacts* to the mental instructional impulse a split second later. The tennis player also knows that there is no sense in his

---

[91] Laura Habbeger, *Op. Cit.*: "I find it wonderful to know that, seeing that visual, auditory and tactile stimuli travel at different speeds, our nervous system also processes them at different speeds, so as to arrive at the sensation of their being simultaneous."

concentrating either on his arm itself, or on the racquet, his manner of holding which is monitored by a consolidated physical memory, which vigilates at the back of his mind leaving him free to keep his eyes on the ball and ensuring that it is the trajectory of the ball itself, and *his foreseeing* of it, that will generate the cerebral impulse that will guide the movement of the arm.

This movement will be completely established *before* it becomes visible.

Predictability is a crucial factor in velocity and agility;[92] for this reason the professional tennis player will have carefully studied his adversary *before* meeting up with him: with the intention of being able, on the basis of plans made through studying him, to serve him his best stroke, which he will have prepared and assimilated in the absence of any performance anxiety or any other psychological pressure. During performance there will be very little to adjust.

Similarly, a Formula One pilot does not make the acquaintance of the trajectory of a dangerous curve in a circuit while he is challenging it at 300 kilometers per hour, because if he has not examined and drawn the trajectory of that curve in his mind well before arriving at it physically (hopefully taking care to study the circuit thoroughly on paper too, *before* the race), when that curve arrives, the ill-prepared pilot might also be a dead pilot. The expert pilot, who knows the course, will dedicate no more than the corner of an eye to following the curve *while* he is negotiating it, but his mind will be well ahead, he will have all the rest of the circuit to think about. Furthermore, those pilots who have the assistance of co-pilots and navigators know very well that the good ones will give instructions *in time.* [93]

---

[92] It is in fact more difficult to catch a fly in the air – which, although moving at a tenth of the speed of a tennis ball, follows unpredictable trajectories – as seen in the studies of Hinze Hogendoorn, assistant professor at the Department of Experimental Psychology, Faculty of Social Sciences, University of Utrecht (*Time and the brain: the illusion of now*; Ted Talk, 2016).

[93] Even conductors do not give the signal to attack to the players when the moment we already need to hear the sound has arrived, but always slightly ahead of time.

Well then: the voice works in exactly the same way, and we knew this well before science was able to measure unto the last *millisecond* the timings of the muscular reactions to the neuronal impulses; and yet, even today, the greater part of singers ignores this elementary fact. The singer is lucky, too, for nothing has a greater level of *predictability* than a score printed in black on white, more often than not as long as a century ago: the singer knows *exactly* what he is going to sing, he has the opportunity of thoroughly preparing himself for the course, and yet often he fails to profit from this advantage and does not send to his brain the efficient *instructions* necessary for his body to react efficiently.

And you can easily see when these instructions are lacking: the singer who is devoid of them tries for a while to stick to the music, to follow everything that is happening all at the same "present" time. But very soon he is groping for help, he tries emergency tactics, encounters anxiety and breathing difficulties, his voice cracks, he sings flat, gets behind the time, becomes a victim of uneasiness and embarrassment which more and more occupy the entire focus of his attention. He will have to *pretend* to be singing whereas in fact he is only suffering, avoiding the blows of fate and passing off *unease* for *pathos;* he will be praying that the piece will come to an end as soon as possible, releasing him before he chalks up too many dishonorable cracked notes, and all the time the pianist continues to feed him innumerable new phrases with a sadism worthy of a circle of Dante's *Inferno*. (And the singer who does not know what we are talking about is only pretending not to know.)

> Second rule: while you are singing, do *not* listen to yourself and do *not* judge the result.

While the singer is emitting a sound – that is, reverberating in his body something that can be heard at the same time from outside – *at that same time* his mind, far from pausing to listen to or, worse, *comment on* the result, should already be *ahead*, imagining the next sound to be made, and in this way *automatically* leaving all performance instructions to the body, which will shortly be receiving them. When the moment arrives for this vowel sound, *well conceived* in advance, the *properly trained* body, ready to react to instructions from the mind, will deal with it by putting it on automatic pilot, while the (good) singer will already be free to let his mind pass on to the next phrase. Let him be always and exclusively concentrated on this *future design*, giving only his peripheral attention – both auditory and muscular – to *checking* the action of the moment; this with the only scope of collecting the information necessary to any eventual routine "updating of the system", which a singer must do *after* having finished singing and not commenting upon it to himself *while* he is singing, otherwise he risks creating for himself a very distracting and therefore dangerous mental "noise".

And so the golden rule of the public transport system is also valid in singing:

> *"Do not talk to the driver!"*

All the more so if the driver is you yourself: do *not* criticize yourself, and keep your eyes *on the road*.

We can never insist too much on the fact that a singer must not be addicted to actively listening to the sound he is making *while* he is producing it, because this attitude – which we might again define *narcissistic*, in that it is based more on the external effect than on the certainty of the genuine quality of the artistic process of the artisan at work – will distract him and therefore lead him to sing flat and become tired, inexpressive, self-referential, unmusical, imprecise. Like someone who, when walking, does not look where he is going, but looks at himself in shop windows to make sure of his appearance: sooner or later he will walk into a lamp-post. One cannot expect good results when the mind is not constantly running ahead, *foreseeing* what has to be done and limiting itself to watching over the present with that *corner of the eye* that is in charge of all muscular automatisms (from changing gear when you are driving, to *unblocking* the screen of your cell-phone).

During the act of singing, let the singer be concentrated on only one kind of listening: *that mental, imagined listening to his own future voice*, or the listening of his own linguistic and musical *inspiration*. Let his body be kept elastic, docile, receptive and as *still* as possible (stillness will be a direct consequence of the deep level of concentration that such interior listening requires). Let it be his body that adapts itself to that vision; let it never be the vision that has to sacrifice itself to human limitations.

Ever since the world began,

> ***it is the idea that forms the technique; not vice-versa.***

The route that the idea follows in becoming reality (sound reality, in this case), with the fewest number possible of compromises, is what we call *technique* (for the Greeks *techné* was already art, not scaffolding for art, as we often consider it today).

Where our interior eyes rest, *there* will our voice be a moment later, without fail and without our having done anything: it will just happen. Get used to this *relationship of trust between thought and body*, consolidate it during practice, take it as certain; then go on with confidence.

Trying to control the sound of your voice by listening to it as it comes out is intuitively a completely useless act, like wanting to change the headlines when the paper has already been printed: an ingenuous and almost infantile gesture. During the present moment we can only physically embrace – through skillful automatisms – *the voice that has been thought out previously* and up to a point one can take care to limit the effects of eventual careless mistakes, where these take place (whenever you have accustomed yourself to being careful, any mistakes will be little ones for which you will easily be able to find a remedy).

Sight misreading

In the light of what has been discussed in this chapter, singing music at first sight is expressly forbidden.

Even in the context of auditions for choral singers the sight-reading test should be eliminated and practicing this should be absolutely discouraged among *all* singers, sacred and profane. From the point of view of choosing who might be suitable for a professional collaboration, it would be better to investigate the manner, the intelligence and the speed with which a singer can *study* the part *before* performing it. To say that someone who is gifted with excellent sight-reading abilities does not play (or sing) so well is not entirely a commonplace: in making music, you must always know what is coming up, in order to have a *pre-vision* that may inspire the gesture.

The greatest improvisers in history (from Bach to Coltrane) already had a global vision of the result before manifesting their own thought in sound: a vision that the poor musician, singer or chorister, cannot have about a piece that, to begin with, he has not composed himself and that, to make matters worse, he has never seen before, and in which he cannot foresee – in the rosiest of cases – any more than one or two bars that he might glimpse out of the corner of his eye immediately before having to begin it: too little, to be sure, and too little to be able to transform them into musical art and good singing, as we have explained above.

VII. Interpretative diction

No words can express the sublime effect of this word as she pronounced it.

Giuseppe Verdi
on Adelina Patti in the rôle of Gilda,
in a letter to Giulio Ricordi, 1877

He was perhaps the only tenor of his day who carried out a profound and constant study of the psychology of the character through analysis of the sung word: weight, colour, expression of every word acquire in him an increased significance, of which he only possessed the secret.

Luciano Pavarotti
on Aureliano Pertile,
in "Pertile, una voce, un mito" by Bruno Tosi

The cavatina: learning *to get through it*

In a preceding chapter, when discussing the uselessness of practising *vocalises* simply to warm up the voice, we mentioned the fact that the composer, together with the librettist, gives the singer, in his *aria di sortita* or *cavatina* [94] (the "opening aria" of a character), the warm-up most suited to carry through the rôle allotted to him. In this last chapter, dealing with the importance of operatic diction for the purposes of interpretation, we think it might be useful to enter more deeply into details of this truth.

We should think of the *cavatina* as the *manifesto* of the character: it is at one and the same time an index of his musical themes, a synopsis of his

---

[94] «At the end of the seventeenth century, a *cavata* was defined as a short melodic phrase in the *arioso* style, which the composer *ri-cava* [carves] from a passage of blank verse. In the eighteenth century, the definition *cavatina* was given to a simple *arietta*, without any *da capo*, composed to one single strophe of text (e.g. *L'ho perduta, me meschina*, sung by Barbarina at the beginning of Act IV of Mozart's *Le nozze di Figaro*, 1786, which even starts off directly without any recitative). In the nineteenth century, the term was no longer used to define one particular musical form, but to designate the aria (in the usual form) that a main character sings on his first appearance onstage (also known as an *aria di sortita*); that means that it also defines its position. With this meaning, solo numbers in Opera inserted into the *Introduzione* (not always in the usual form) were often referred to as *cavatina*.»; Lorenzo Bianconi and Giorgio Pagannone, *Piccolo glossario di drammaturgia musicale*.

scenic antecedents, a snapshot of his psychology, a hint of his evolution. Therefore it constitutes, in general, a kind of *Bildungsroman*[95]: the outset of his sentimental and vocal education, arming him for the rôle and featuring all the indispensable premises towards facing it.

Think of the evolution of the *three voices* of Violetta – one for each act – all three permeated, to a greater or lesser degree, with the tubercular rasp that gradually worsens. Think of the young ballerina Gilda warming up at the bar, using her nightingale's voice with sublime grace, dancing on points on the vowels of the *Caro nome* – the name dearest to her – as if she were a schoolgirl scribbling her name entwined with that of her beloved in her diary; and yet that name is false (this emphasizes even more for us her fragile purity and her desperate innocence). Think of the lofty and at the same time furtive legato of Norma, who fools her entire war-thirsty tribe into waiting with a sacred ritual (which itself has its deceitful side), with the only aim of saving the object of her love. Think of the masterly skill of Rosina – who has no further need of teachers (or *tutors*: after speaking to her, Figaro will say to himself: *Ve', che bestia! Il maestro faccio a lei!*) [96] – to let loose and to escape unharmed from the *cento trappole*[97] that Rossini sets her, right from her first appearance onstage, with the idea of showing the audience the astuteness of this *volpe sopraffina*[98] and novice of love. (In Italian, *Una voce poco fa* may also mean, without too much stretching, that *una voce fa poco*, which means "to have a nice voice is not enough").

Making up an imaginative etymology, we might posit that a character's entrance aria is called a *cavatina* because it drills a singer to literally *cavarsela* (in Italian, "get through, cope with the difficulties") in his rôle and onstage life, demonstrating right from the beginning (above all to himself, so as to get the necessary dose of self-confidence) whether he has all that it takes to tackle the part.

And as we will clearly see in the next paragraph, treating what is possibly the most famous *cavatina* of all times, there is no way to get through such a test without complete mastery of the diction.

---

[95] A novel dealing with one person's formative years or spiritual education.
[96] "What an ass I am, teaching *her* something!".
[97] "A hundred vocal traps".
[98] "Sly fox".

The Rossini neurosis

Try to say aloud, very quickly:

> *Qua la sanguigna,*
> *presto, la barba,*
> *presto il biglietto!*

And then, even more quickly:

> *Lancette e forbici,*
> *rasori e pettini,*
> *al mio comando*
> *tutto qui sta.*

Ah yes, it's difficult: you need a tongue as tripping as Figaro's, the barber of Seville. Here we have the most classic stereotype of a barber: who always knows everything about everybody, better than anyone at smarming up to a client, extorting from him very private information while, when necessary, assuming the rôle of psychologist and doctor (and *chirurgo, botanico, spezial, veterinario...*[99]), with one eye on the client's beard, the other on the street and his tongue wagging all over the place.

Figaro is of less than modest origin – we simply don't know, until the end of the second play in Beaumarchais's trilogy,[100] when it is discovered that he is the son of Marcellina and Bartolo – and yet this foundling, emblem of the nascent *bourgeoisie*, is full of ambitions, to satisfy which he must depend exclusively on his wits, sharpened daily – together with his razor – on that hard stone which we would call the *school of life*. He thrives only on *the volcano of his mind*, depending for his maintenance on his quickness of thought in sniffing out a bargain and on the dexterity of his tongue in convincing the client of the moment to conclude it (even the *genialotta* [101] Rosina says of him: "Yes, I spoke to him: I like him, he is nice, he pleases me with his chat").

---

[99] "In this house I am surgeon, botanist, apothecary, veterinary..."; Cesare Sterbini, libretto of *Il Barbiere di Siviglia*, Act I.

[100] Pierre-Augustin Caron de Beaumarchais (Paris, 24 January 1732 - Paris, 18 May 1799) was a French dramatist and controversialist. His Figaro trilogy consists of *Le Barbier de Séville*, *Le Mariage de Figaro* and *La Mère Coupable*.

[101] "Pleasantly plump."

Every time that he gets what he wants, thanks to his seductive charm, he is pleased with himself: but, at the same time, every *invenzione prelibata*,[102] every *mostro singular* [103] generated by his mind, almost frightens and overwhelms him, also because it is impossible to satisfy all the requests they give rise to.

(Each, but I mean each allusion such as: *Tutti mi vogliono: donne e ragazzi; V'è la risorsa, poi, del mestiere: colla donnetta, laranlallera... col cavaliere, laranlallà; A tutti, non so perché, m'adatto a far piacere; Là, senza fallo, mi troverà; Eh via, pulisciti il bocchino*[104] makes it perfectly clear that already at the dawn of the nineteenth century the figure of the hair stylist radiated a certain sexually exuberant and ambiguous je ne sais quoi.)

The twenty-five-year-old Rossini could not but have seen himself in this figure of an *extraordinarily endowed* young man who, one moment after being galvanized by his own *bravura,* collapses under the weight of his own excesses and starts imploring *uno alla volta, per carità!* [105] Rossini had just given birth to one of history's greatest masterpieces and he was drawing understandably nearer to the serious nervous breakdown that would accompany him for the rest of his life.

Let us now add sound to this psychological profile: imagine the protagonist speaking with a marked *Romagnolo* [106] *accent*, as Figaro must of course have been conceived by his young father (nicknamed *il cigno di Pesaro* ("the swan of Pesaro") by his contemporaries, the Maestro quipped that he felt himself

---

[102] "Exquisite invention".

[103] "Singular monstrosity".

[104] "They all want me: ladies and youths, old men and girls"; "Then there's the resources of the job: with the young lady *laranlallera*... with the young gentleman...*laranlallà!*"; "I don't know why, I adapt myself to please them all"; "There you'll find me, make no mistake" (but *fallo* in Italian also means *phallus*); "Now then, wipe your mouth clean" (but *bocchino* in Italian also means *fellatio*).

[105] "One at a time, for heaven's sake!".

[106] Romagna is the East part of Emilia-Romagna, a vast region of northern Italy having as its capital Bologna (the city where the composer attended the conservatory).

to be rather *il cignale* [107] *di Lugo* [108] ("the wild boar of Lugo") – *et voilà*: you have the complete picture. *Largo al factotum* [109] before he bowls us all over.

Yes, because, as our non-Italian reader may understandably not know, few Italian dialects are so rapidly spoken as that of Romagna, which is so fast as to have to contract many vowels to keep up with its own internal metronome, consequently becoming very rhythmical, because, at that speed, intelligibility will all depend on the gunfire of tonic accents and the rhythm. The genius of the Romagnolo people, their exuberance – as authentic as a good bottle of Sangiovese and who, not by accident, have a great passion for *motors* and speed– comes out strongly in their phenomenal velocity of speech.

Well, Rossini raises the curtain on his protagonist with an unequivocable, fast "*la ran la lera, la ran la là*". An authentic *manifesto;* going, from a dramaturgical point of view, beyond a manifestation of joyousness describing the personality of the character and, from a technical-vocal point of view, beyond the voice-warming vocalizzo typical of the *cavatina* (the entrance aria of a character). If Rossini baptizes the appearance of Figaro with a *tongue-twister* it is precisely to demonstrate his *flexibility of tongue*, or to immediately represent his dexterity in everything: his mental and therefore linguistic *agility;* one might say: his *existential* agility.

Largo al factotum della città / presto a bottega che l'alba è già [110], writes Sterbini[111]: *largo,* but *presto;* a curious contradiction in terms and musical *tempi*: as if here even a *largo* were a *presto*. Moreover the singer's tongue must also move rather *presto,* for him to come out unscathed from this imitative *cavatina,* which is the psychological portrait of a hyperactive person (as well as being Rossini's visiting card, who with the *Barbiere* presents himself to the world, though very young, as a gigantic genius and a pillar of the history of music).

---

[107] In the dialect of Romagna, *zignale* /tsignale/ (*cinghiale*, in Italian), means "wild boar"; the pun is on the similarity of *zignale* and *zigno*, /tsigno/ (*cigno*, in Italian), that instead means "swan": Rossini pointed out how, given his corpulence and beyond all flatteries, he looked more like a wild boar than a swan.

[108] Lugo di Romagna, Rossini's father's birthplace, where Gioachino grew up.

[109] "Make way for the factotum". In the word *factotum* there is, given the speed of the aria, a doubling: c+t → tt, hence *factotum* → fattɔtum.

[110] "Make room for the town factotum / get to your shop quickly for dawn is already here."

[111] Cesare Sterbini (Rome, 1784 - Rome, 19 January 1831) was an Italian writer and librettist.

Analyzing the Romagna dialect or any other equally rapid dialect under an acoustic magnifying glass, we realize that when speaking it there is absolutely no time, at such speed, to fully form the vocalic volumes: the Romagnoli must be content, in order that the text should be intelligible, to give priority to the tonic vowels, which will be slightly longer (but not all of them, within a phrase, as we shall see), whereas the atonic vowels will be no more than sketched in and all of them more or less made a *schwa /ə/*. Let us take the example of a born and bred Romagnolo who, to the question "what did you do last night?" replies *eh, sono stato a casa* ("oh, I stayed at home"): in effect, he would say *schən stat'ə kajə* – only one tonic vowel fully enunciated out of three; total time employed in the utterance: less than a second.

The understanding of this phenomenon, which we shall here extemporarily baptize as *vocalic reduction*, is very useful to us to understand how to manage, from the linguistic point of view, the *neurotic* tempi of a Rossini score: it shows us how Rossini *felt* those words that he then set to music (since, if he set them to music the way he did, it is obvious that he thought them this way in his head and his linguistic background could not fail to be a decisive factor in his creative processes).

The text of *Largo al factotum* will be found below with, beside it, its orthoepic diction; once you have got used to it, just by trying to read it aloud, you will already notice how much the time saved by *vocalic reduction* makes pronunciation smoother, Rossini's wild tempi more natural and everything more singable. Notice how, in some particularly fast phrases, even some secondary tonic vowels in the phrase are reduced to *schwa*: at this high speed, the phrasing is thought of more broadly, and will leave space, in the end, for one single tonic vowel to be fully formed within the whole phrase.

Study the piece like this and then, setting yourself a comfortable speed (or, you might say, taking the *largo* within the *presto*), put back, wherever possible, the real vowels, but consider that, even without them, the listener however will be able to understand everything, sometimes even more so, and always more than he would if the singer began to struggle through fatigue (which would, indeed, be far from *Figaresque*) in the vain attempt to catch them all *a tempo*. Let it be remembered that this cavatina, however fine and famous, is a mere *aperitif* for the baritone: the real stuff comes

Interpretative diction | 115

afterwards; it would be better not to get too tired when you have only just stepped onto the stage.

For this reason we now ask the reader to venture with *great* patience upon reading and understanding the *cavatina* in question, as we have copied it out in the right-hand column, that is, in its phonetic and orthoepic version, annotated according to the symbols already specified and explained in this manual. After a first glance, which we hope will not make it seem too difficult, a new world will be revealed to him (and, if the reader is a singer who has struggled with this aria for years without *getting through it* or getting himself out of it, we guarantee that he will find in what follows the key to resolving a lifetime of vocal problems).

In the extreme speed of enunciation of this so typically *Romagnolo* text, the vast majority of atonic vowels will turn into *schwa* and many clashes of two different consonants will be assimilated into doublings. Furthermore, we have indicated in heavy black only and exclusively the vowels that must be preserved in their entirety in diction, and we have also underlined them, as they are, intuitively, all tonic vowels: just as we have also recommended you to do earlier on in the book; the purpose of this is to suggest that the reader give these vowels a greater volume of sound than to the rest of the verse, the volume of which should be reduced almost to nothing in the study phase. The singer should act as though he had a volume control knob for his own voice, like old stereo players or car radios do: a knob that, at a turn of the wrist, can suddenly raise and lower the volume. In this way the reader will apply a greater wave of vocal energy only to the tonic vowels indicated, making them instantly stand out from all the rest: thanks to this trick, the tongue will move freely, relaxed and without tension within this labyrinth which, after a few tries – this is guaranteed – will no longer be as impenetrable as it may seem at present.

So, be brave and give it a try!

| *La ran la lera, la ran la là!*
Largo al factotum Della città, largo!
La ran la, la ran la, la ran la - là!
Presto a bottega ché l'alba è già, presto! | llərənləll**e**ra* llərənləll**a***
ll**a**rgəlfətt**ao**tumdəlləcətt**a**ll**a**rgo*
llərənl**a**llərənl**a**llrənl**a**ll**a***
ppr**æ**stəbətt**e**gakəllə(l)bəggi**a**ppr**æ**sto* |

La ran la, la ran la, la ran la - là!	llərənlallərənlallərənlalla*
Ah, che bel vivere,	akkebbæləvivəre*
Che bel piacere,	kkebbæləpiacere*
Per un barbier	pperunəbarəbiærə*
Di qualità, di qualità!	ddiqualitaddiqualita*
Ah, bravo, Figaro,	abbrəvəffigərə
Bravo, bravissimo - bravo!	bbravəbbravissəməbbravo*
Fortunatissimo, Per verità - bravo!	ffortənətissəmoppə(r)vveritabbravo*
Fortunatissimo, Per verità!	ffortunatissiməpperəverita*
Pronto a far tutto,	pprə(n)təffərətuttə
La notte e il giorno	llənəttələgəəorna
Sempre d'intorno	sæ(m)pprədəntorənə
In giro sta.	əngirəsta*
Miglior cuccagna,	mməgləkkəkkagnə
Per un barbiere,	ppərəbbəbbiærə*
Vita più nobile,	vvitəpiənnaobələ
No, non si dà.	nnaonnəssəda*
La ran la, la ran la, la ran la - là!	llərəllərəllələrllella*
Rasori e pettini	rrəzəreppættənə
Lancette e forbici	ləncettəffaobbəcə
Al mio comando	əlməkəma(n)də
Tutto qui sta.	ttəttəquəsta*
V'è la risorsa, poi, del mestiere	vvællarisorsa* ppaoidelmestiære*
Colla donnetta, Col cavaliere...	kkolladonnetta* kkoləkavaliære*
Colla donnetta... La ran la lera	kkolladonnetta* llərənləllera*
Col cavaliere... La ran la là - là là, là	kkoləkavaliære* llərənlləlla* lla* lla*
Ah, che bel vivere...	akkebbæləvivəre...
Tutti mi chiedono	ttəttəməkəædənə*
Tutti mi vogliono	ttəttəməvaoglənə*
Donne, ragazzi,	ddaonnərrəgazzi*
Vecchi, fanciulli:	vvækkiffəncəullə*

Qua la parrucca...	qquəlləpərr**u**kkə*
Presto la barba...	ppər**æ**stələb**a**rəbə*
Qua la sanguigna...	qquələsəngu**i**nnə*
Presto il biglietto...	ppr**æ**stəbbilləə**e**ttə*
Ehi, Figaro! Figaro	**e**əff**i**garo*
(Figaro, Figaro, Figaro!)	ff**i**garo*(ff**i**gərəff**i**gərəff**i**garo*)
Ahimè, che furia!	aim**æ*** aim**æ**kkəff**u**riə*
Ahimè, che folla!	aim**æ*** kkəff**o**llə*
Uno alla volta, Per carità!	**u**nəalləv**o**ltapperkarit**a***
Ehi, Figaro! - Son qua.	**e**i* ff**i**gərə* ssəqqu**a***
Figaro qua, Figaro là,	ff**i**gərəqu**a**ffigərəll**a***
Figaro su, Figaro giù	ff**i**gərəs**u**gigərəggə**u***
Pronto prontissimo,	pprəttəprətt**i**ssəmə
Son come il fulmine:	ssəkkəmələff**o**mmənə
Sono il factotum della città.	ssənəffətt**a**otəm
Della città! Della città!	ddəlləcətt**a**ddəlləcətt**a***
Ah, bravo Figaro! Bravo, bravissimo...	əbbrəvəff**i**gərəbbrəvəbbərəv**i**ssəmə...*
A te fortuna non mancherà.	əttəffətt**u**nənnəmməkkər**a***

There you are: in this way, even after the first attempt at a reading it sounds much better and makes much more sense, don't you think?

Cæsar *docet*

We hardly know who were the literary figures who inconvenienced themselves by writing libretti for the operas whose lines we have been singing by heart for ever – turning back yet again to Fellini's words opening this treatise[112]; words that bear witness to the structural importance of

---

[112] «...Opera is part of my Italian nature, just like the bersaglieri, Garibaldi, the Roman emperors. *Celeste Aida, Questa o quella per me pari sono, Stride la vampa*: these voices have always accompanied us. I have always had them in my ears. We have seen all our aunts and their daughters weeping into their hand-made lace while they sang *Mi chiamano Mimì* and our uncles while they roared out, passionately *Se quel guerrier io fossi*. These things belong to us so much that they become estranged, as is the subconscious.»; Federico Fellini, *Op. Cit.*

Opera in the constitution of the Italian nation: a new Olympus of mythological figures cut out to measure for the new nation, new and immortal interpreters of the archetypes of the national collective subconscious. Even singers rarely venture beyond the indispensable figures (like Metastasio, Da Ponte and Piave) to pass their examination in History of Music and Poetic and Dramatic Literature (hoping that they are indeed still indispensable). And yet, in the dawn of Opera, consistently with the *manifesto* declared by Peri in the preface to *Euridice*, quoted above more than once[113], it was the poet's name and not the composer's that took first place on the score. Today the names of the librettists are conspicuous by their absence even from the covers of the vocal and full scores of the leading music publishers; as a result, even when names like Giacosa, Illica, Cammarano or Ghislanzoni may ring a bell – if it is only an eidetic memory arising from a glance, whether at a page or at the television screen or whatever, because they collaborated on operas that are constantly studied, performed or broadcast – there are people who already get lost when faced with Sterbini, while with regard to other names they are completely in the dark. Giuseppe Adami: a genius, a modern lyricist of an Opera conceived in terms cinematic rather than theatrical (such as Puccini's opera is, with its zoomings, its camera shots within one and the same crowded place, masterfully connecting characters and lines that have no apparent connection, its magical lighting effects all created by the music); or the Abbé Varesco: a Latinist, whose mother tongue was not even Italian, with a passion for linguistic *puzzles* – to name just two.

The name of Nicola Francesco Haym[114], then, might will give rise to the proverbial *Carneade! Who was he?*[115] Well, here goes: he was an Italian of

---

[113] «...the idea was to imitate the spoken word with singing [...] so that harmony, enhancing that of everyday speech, should arise from melody, from singing, so as to form something between the two.»; Jacopo Peri, *Op. Cit.*

[114] C.f. note 77

[115] From the *Enciclopedia Treccani*: «**Carnèade** [noun. m.] [from the name of the Greek philosopher Carneade (214 -129 B.C.), alluding to the beginning of chapter 8 of Alessandro Manzoni's novel *I Promessi Sposi*, in which Don Abbondio asks himself, upon finding the name in a book he is reading: "Carneade! Who was he?"] (used only in the singular). – An unknown person, never heard of: *for me he is a c.; I'm sure that some c. or other will be elected.*»

German descent, a 'cellist in Arcangelo Corelli's[116] orchestra, for which he composed cantatas and oratorios; in 1700 he moved to London where he translated and had numerous Italian operas performed and later came to know Georg Friedrich Händel, for whom he wrote numerous librettos, among which the marvelous one for *Giulio Cesare in Egitto*, which, more than an opera, constitutes one of the earliest examples of a *Broadway style musical*, in which the recitatives carry the story forward and the *songs* serve the purpose of being sung by the *virtuosi* and by the audience[117] and so swelling the box-office takings. We want to pause a while here to consider this libretto, since it is so valid from every point of view in underlining various fundamental aspects of poetry meant to be set to music.

In particular, on various occasions this libretto proves the truth of a cardinal principle of dramaturgy, and that is that

no verse is there by chance.

On stage, *if a word were of no use, it would not be spoken*. If it has been written, there *must* be a reason: to synthesize what happened before the rise of the curtain, to allude to hidden truths or bring them forth, to define a relationship, to provoke a quarrel (or a war), to make clear an understanding, to paint a character's portrait or to mock him; sometimes it will even be said just to lie or to dissimulate; but, in any case, if that word has been chosen and deposited there, it is because it has a precise dramaturgical value and it is a clue to *a something*. It is up to the interpreter's skill to ferret it out.

We shall quote some verses taken from *Giulio Cesare* which at first sight one might judge as minor, negligible, of the kind that might be cut out and which, in fact, often are cut out of the great mass of recitatives in so long an opera;

---

[116] Arcangelo Corelli (Fusignano, 17 February 1653 - Rome, 8 January 1713) was an Italian violinist and composer, considered one of the leading figures of baroque music.

[117] Giovanni Battista Draghi, known as Pergolesi (Fermo, 1710 - Pozzuoli, 1736), in his *Stabat Mater*, dating from the year in which the young composer died, therefore only 12 years after Händel's opera, inserts a contralto aria (*Fac ut portem*) that is shamelessly modeled on an aria of Cornelia (*Nel tuo seno*): the same *alto* register, the same key of G minor, the same rhythmic movement, the same melody in the strings. This is a sign that the arias in *Giulio Cesare* must have entered into the *koiné* very quickly, like real *hits*.

and yet every one of them contains nothing less than a universe, if you know how to bless them with a correct reading, duly conveyed to the audience.

The first verse that we shall examine belongs to Nireno, a minor character, servant of Cleopatra; it is a phrase that he addresses, in fact, to his mistress and it is nothing more than a simple, fleeting, apparently insignificant "*Non ti scoprir!*". ("Do not give yourself away!"). It is the scene[118] in which Cleopatra decides to reveal herself to Cornelia and Sesto with a view to encouraging the boy to avenge the death of his father by killing the perverse Tolomeo – her brother and therefore a rival claimant to the throne of Egypt. From the wings, where she has been overhearing the conversation between mother and son, upon hearing Sesto's timorous question "*Ma, oh Dio! Chi al re fellone ci scorterà?*"[119], the queen rushes onstage *ex machina* and answers him with a triumphant "*Cleopatra!*", promptly suppressed by Nireno with the *Non ti scoprir!* that we are discussing: an admonition which the queen seems to obey, covering up her slip by adding "*...e Lidia ancora [...] Sotto nome di Lidia io servo a Cleopatra: se in virtù del tuo braccio ascende al trono, sarai felice e scorgerai qual sono!*"[120]. It looks, therefore, as though, upon Nireno's rebuke, Cleopatra denies being the queen herself, immediately after having given herself away.

---

[118] CORNELIA. Take heart, my son, be brave! I shall follow you courageously.

SESTO. But! (Oh God!) Who will lead us to the guilty king?

CLEOPATRA: [Appearing suddenly] Cleopatra!

NIRENO: **Do not give yourself away!**

CLEOPATRA: And Lidia too, who, in order that the evil man be dethroned, will shield you, and lead you to him.

CORNELIA: And what impels you, friendly girl, to offer yourself in our aid today?

CLEOPATRA: The guilt of a tyrannical king, and right. Under the name of Lidia I serve Cleopatra; if she gains the throne through your help, you will be happy and discover who I am.

CORNELIA: Who will lead us?

CLEOPATRA: This man, a faithful servant of the queen, will be able to cautiously lead you to the great undertaking.

SESTO: He is no son, who does not avenge his father's death. I shall draw my sword, and the great tyrant of Egypt will be struck down and fall."

Nicola Francesco Haym, libretto of *Giulio Cesare in Egitto*, Act I.

[119] "But, oh heaven, who will lead us to the wicked king?"

[120] "... and Lidia too... Under the name of Lidia I serve Cleopatra: if she gains the throne through your help, you will be happy, and see who I am!".

This scene is crucial, the one deciding the outcome of the opera, yet it is often misunderstood both by singers and directors. Sesto is a boy who was a child only yesterday (his mother still calls him *viscere mie* ("child of my womb"), having only recently lost his great father Pompeo, whose head he has just now seen offered on a plate to Cesare by Tolomeo; his mother Cornelia, a noble lady of great beauty, finding herself in a foreign country where *barbarians* seek to entice her at every opportunity, is so desperate that she has tried to commit suicide by stealing her son's knife, and now there she is, distraught with grief: and to make matters worse, the spirit of Pompeo, invoked by the dismayed boy during his first aria – *Svegliatevi nel core, furie d'un alma offesa, a far d'un traditore aspra vendetta!* [121] – has told the boy that he himself will have to go and kill the *villain* in whose palace mother and son now find themselves, defenceless prisoners (*L'ombra del genitore accorre a mia difesa e dice: 'a te il rigor, figlio, s'aspetta!'*).[122] All that remains is for Sesto to pick up the courage to act, in other words. The boy wants to have a try, wants to hold high his august father's name, but he seems undecided, also because, if something were to go wrong, it would all be over for both of them. For these reasons he needs a god to come down from above in his aid, to arm him with noble strength, while assuring his success; that god will be – *dans le bleu* – Cleopatra in the scene mentioned above. There is, however, a problem: finding yourself in an enemy palace in which even the walls have ears, how can you believe what the first comer says, especially if soberly dressed, who tells you that she is the queen (or sent by her) and then *nonchalantly* orders you to go and kill the master of the house, furthermore only allowing you an unarmed eunuch as escort? Not only would the simple declaration "*Cleopatra!*" not have been enough to certify the queen's identity, but it would rather have aroused suspicions in the two Romans: and so the *Non ti scoprir!* of the queen's faithful servant turns out to be absolutely *crucial* to telling her two terrified interlocutors who she is – while it makes her introduction, which has happened anyway, look like a frivolity on the part of a woman who has every reason to protect herself by maintaining her incognito. Her continuing to pass herself off as Lidia throughout the scene is at that point certainly not intended, on the queen's part, to delude Sesto

---

[121] "Awaken in my breast, furies of a wounded soul, to wreak vengeance on a traitor!".

[122] "The shade of my father rushes to my aid and says: 'my son, punishment is up to you!'"

and Cornelia into thinking that she is *really* Lidia, but rather to make them think that they are dealing with a person of such importance that she ought not to have given herself away – but never mind, now the thing is done and "if she [Cleopatra] gains the throne through your help, you will be happy and discover who I am", winking away at the boy, who, at this point, has understood and suddenly makes up his mind: "I shall draw my sword, and the great tyrant of Egypt will be struck down and fall."

If we want to look further into it, we cannot believe either, considering the famous political acumen of the Egyptian queen, that her revealing herself to the Roman couple could have been due to carelessness, and so we must also suppose that Nireno's *Non ti scoprir!* is a trick of theatrical legerdemain, well rehearsed by the queen and her servant, to be used when called for. This is how a little three-word phrase, placed furthermore in the mouth of a servant, and let drop furtively, in a whisper, contains all at the same time a vast quantity of information: the proof of friendship between a servant and an intelligent queen (moreover, an enlightened ruler: the rapport between the two is proof of the intelligence and open-mindedness of both parties and, on this basis, of their equal dignity and great complicity; different indeed from the relationship between Tolomeo and his yet faithful general Achilla, who will be nonetheless betrayed by the tyrant). Lastly, it also tells us how solving the most intricate of palace plots and sometimes the fate of entire nations is always entrusted to women and servants: Cesare, in fact, with all his valour and all his ardour for the queen (whom he will later marry), will never manage to pull a hair out of Tolomeo's beard and, rather, will run the risk of being killed. If it had not been for those three providential little words of Nireno's, that propel young Sesto to commit regicide, things would have turned out very badly for everyone.

That Cesare and Cleopatra are made for each other we can understand from their mutual mental and therefore vocal agility, a characteristic that, as we saw above when talking about Figaro, is *always* a symptom of extreme brilliance and rapidity of thought (in the early chapters of this book it is explained in detail how in order to sing well one must know how to *think well*: in advance, in good time and *a tempo*. The only three agile voices in this opera are, not by chance, those of the two starring lovers and that of the young Sesto. Cornelia will acquire agility and respite only in her last aria (*Non ha più che temere, quest'alma vendicata, or sì, sarà beata, comincio a *respirar!* – "My soul, now avenged, has nothing more to fear, yes, now it will be blessed, I can breathe again!": however the agility here is moderate, calm, and never electric like that of the other three), after the enterprising spirit of Cleopatra has pervaded and influenced her, freeing her from the sorrow that was weighing her down and from her rigid and impotent gravity. Tolomeo and Achilla, on their part, have, of course, some agility passages, but of quite another kind (the agility for the former, suggesting the tantrums of a spoiled child, is more reduced and more rhetorical than that of the main characters; that of the latter is scholastic, clumsy, almost obtuse, in speaking brutally of love to Cornelia after having cut her beloved husband's head off, as on other occasions; agility that a *yes-man* might have, in other words).

Cesare and Cleopatra, moreover, share an animal instinct for situations and people, may they be either friends or enemies (only by a son of his own,[123] in whom he therefore blindly trusted, would it be possible for Cæsar to be betrayed one day). This kind of intelligence we might well define as *sexual* in its nature: in classical culture, which was embodied in the Latin Caesar, sexuality was notoriously (and let us here suspend any kind of ethical judgment influenced by our society of today, which furthermore is no less *barbarous* than others past and present, in many aspects) an essential component in children's education, when aiming at a holistic development of their intelligence and personality. This was, at one and the same time, a physical, emotional, spiritual and intellectual training towards logical-deductive thought on a basis that is empirical, pragmatic, experimental, *sensual* – of the senses: this education was the foundation of the monumental classical Greek culture and therefore of the Latin one, too.

An infinite number of times throughout the opera it is remarked, above all by the *alta* ("high born") *Cornelia* (who, as we are informed by Cesare, is *gran germe de' Scipioni* ("a noble offspring of the Scipio family"[124] – that is, a descendant of one of the most noble Roman families) when she is repeatedly harassed by Tolomeo, how any union between Romans and *barbarians*[125] was

---

[123] Marcus Junius Brutus (85 BC - 23 October 42 BC), often referred to simply as Brutus, was a Roman senator and the most famous of the assassins of Julius Cæsar, who believed Brutus to be a biological son of his.

[124] An important patrician family of ancient Rome, belonging to the *gens Cornelia*.

[125] The Greek term *barbaròs* comes from the onomatopoeia *bar-bar*, mimicking and incomprehensible utterance, a "barking", and was therefore quite offensive.

considered inconceivable, even when the barbarian was of royal blood. Yet Cleopatra, *barbarian* though she be, makes an exception to this rule and may aspire to Cesare because, as her vocal writing demonstrates, she shares his qualities of thought and his spirit, which is not fatalist at all, but rather determined: how different from her brother Tolomeo, who, in his first diplomatic meeting with Cesare, goes so far as to reduce his unstoppable *Veni, vidi, vici* to a mere concession of the blindfolded goddess: *Cesare, alla tua destra stende fasci di scettri generosa la Sorte!*[126] – another unusually significant line carrying two entire cultural systems: this fatalism of Tolomeo's would seem to be a symptom not only of the character's narcissistic presumption, but also of his superstition and cultural backwardness.

But even inside this very Roman encampment not all men are equal and Haym, once again, does not fail to make use of apparently casual phrases that, however, are of striking effect, if properly understood and properly pronounced, in delineating not only the characters to whom they are entrusted, but also those to whom they are addressed, as well as third parties. Here the librettist's intention is certainly to portray right from the start the superiority and moral integrity of the title-rôle in comparison with any of the others.

In the opening scene, Cesare is depicted contemplating the Egypt that he has just conquered, and beside him stands his right-hand man, Curio, of whom this already tells us that he is a man of valour (and in fact he will stay near to the commander all through the opera, saving his life and risking his own). Well, this same valiant Curio, while he is congratulating Cesare on the lightning victory – *Tu qui, signor, giungesti a tempo, appunto, a prevenir le trame* [127] – noticing a beautiful woman drawing near the scene, does not hesitate to brusquely change the subject, exclaiming: "*Ma chi ver noi sen viene?*", which literally means: "But who is this that approaches us?".

Upon this apparently simple "*Ma chi ver noi sen viene?*" we should like to dwell and propose a series of hypotheses, following clues.

We ask ourselves: could Curio's be simple curiosity – and the reader will excuse the play on words – that is: could Curio *actually* be simply wondering

---

[126] "Caesar, a generous fate offers bunches of scepters to your hand".
[127] "Sir, you got here just in time to forestall plots".

and asking aloud who the person is who is approaching the scene? If you think about it, well, no: because usually when a character comes on stage, he just does it, and that's that: after which, either he comes forward spontaneously, or performs an action that introduces him, or somebody speaks to him and in some way we find out who he is. So, what is the dramaturgical scope of this *Ma chi ver noi sen viene?* that accompanies the onstage entrance of the mysterious female character? Moreover, Cesare gives Curio a sharp reply to his question: "*Questa è Cornelia.*";[128] which gives rise to further suspicions about the function of Curio's question, insomuch as underlings do not usually ask questions of their superiors, but rather the contrary.

Our hypothesis is that Curio's question is entirely rhetorical and that its sense is not to be found in the literal meaning of the phrase: Curio has spotted lovely female contours in the distance and, changing the subject from politics to more *matey* matters, would like to share this information with his leader and friend, adding a further colourful note to the relationship between the two men. Furthermore, that Cornelia is beautiful enough to stand out even at a distance is confirmed by a myriad of other lines, during the course of the opera, and by several characters, including even Cleopatra: she is objectively beautiful, then, which leads us to think that *Ma chi ver noi sen viene?* might well be one way of saying "*Just look there...and who can she be?*"; men's talk, a perfect delineation of soldiers at war, in other words. But the abrupt *Questa è Cornelia* that Curio gets from Cesare is no less significant: Cesare pours cold water on his man's enthusiasm; unlike his underling, he does not view sexually the lady whose bearing declares her nobility from afar – this is so much the case that he recognizes her and calls her by her name. Cesare's answer, therefore, tells us how the Latin *vir*,[129] the real man of valour, does not let himself be overwhelmed by feminine fascinations, which immediately sets a great moral distance between him and Curio (anticipating that Cesare's forthcoming passion for Cleopatra, though containing a strong component of physical and sexual attraction, is eminently founded on affinities, as we have already stressed).

---

[128] "This is Cornelia."

[129] *Vir* (Lat. *vir, viri* - "male, man") in Roman culture was not a simple male individual, but a man of value and *virtue* (the etymon is mutual).

The remaining part of the rapid exchange that introduces the entrance of Cornelia removes any doubts that we might have had about the nature of Curio's question, for he follows Cesare's answer by saying: "*Oh sorte, del nemico Pompeo l'alta consorte? Cesare: a questa un tempo sacrai la libertade.*" ("Oh destiny! Our enemy Pompeo's noble consort? Cæsar: long ago I fell in love with her."). Curio had been so carried away by his baser instincts as to not have recognized a woman whom he had once loved.

This is how the apparently rhetorical "*Ma chi ver noi sen viene?*", if clearly articulated, serves to inform us, at the outset, about many facts: that Cesare, apart from being brave, is also lucid, moral and incorruptible, in contrast with his underlings, even when men of value; that, if Curio has had past dealings with a noble lady such as Cornelia, he must be more or less a man of good taste and not like those who run after the first woman they see; that Cornelia is a woman of great beauty and will therefore be horribly molested by all the men, to the point of being sick unto death of it all (when she is taken to Tolomeo's palace and is wooed by him and rejects him, the tyrant orders her to be sent as a punishment to the gardens of the harem *a coltivare i fiori* ("to cultivate flowers"): another apparently innocuous little phrase, but *strongly* significant, for growing flowers is not limited to being a humble occupation, especially if imposed on an aristocrat, but it is also carried out in a humiliating and sexually exposed position: a master would only have to draw near and take his pleasure at will).

The unfortunate Cornelia had come onstage (too late, alas) to beg Cesare to make an armistice with the troops of her husband Pompeo, who has ill-advisedly allied himself with the barbarian Tolomeo against his fellow-citizen (not a nice thing to do, between one Roman and another: and yet Pompeo was highly respected and nearly all Rome was for him, viewing Cesare with malevolence) in the hope that, together, they might wrest Egypt from him. Cornelia suspects, with the good wife's infallible sixth sense, that something has happened, because Pompeo has probably not come home in the night: her adored husband has, in fact, been betrayed and murdered by his barbarian ally, who had the vague idea of using his severed head as a welcome offering to Cesare… but all in vain, because, appalled by the horrific sight, Cesare speedily fulminates Tolomeo's messenger Achilla with "*Empio, dirò tu sei, togliti agli occhi miei, sei tutto crudeltà*" ("I'll expose you as impious, get out of my sight, you are all cruelty"); for the audience has to grasp clearly, right from the beginning of the opera, another great concept: that Cesare, the Roman, faced with the severed head of a fellow-citizen – even of one who had tried to betray him and may have been aiming at killing him – does not forget that he is descended from Aeneas, founder of the *caput mundi* and emblem of *pietas*,[130] a value of which the *hybris*[131] of the barbarians is the exact opposite. *Pious* versus *impious* men: in other words, the civil and humane versus the uncivilized and inhuman; and let it be clear to the audience which is which from the start (whoever these two parties might end up representing on stage either back in Händel's day, or in a modern staging).

Cesare does not merely respect his dead fellow-citizen, however much his enemy, and defend and protect his family, but there is even a scene in which he *speaks* to Pompeo, so conferring upon him the dignity of a living and present person; something that, apart from him, only the departed's son Sesto will do, in the scene already mentioned in which the boy invokes his father's spirit (who does not fail to materialize, and through his son's mouth express his will, thus putting a match to the plot). In the presence of an urn containing the ashes of Pompeo, Caesar is the soloist in a lovely accompanied recitative, very intimate and rather long: a monologue of a Hamletic stamp in which, reflecting upon the unexpected end of his great rival, he questions himself on the meaning of his own existence, especially in view of the transient nature of life (the subsequent appearance of the sexy Cleopatra will look like an answer to all his existential questions). Here is another element that our magnificent librettist makes use of to note the *refined sensitivity* of the greatest conqueror in western history: he is so highly perceptive and spiritually evolved as to be able to sense the presence of *spirits*.

Caesar notoriously had infallible intuition and, far from being an *macho* icon, he succeeded in the most incredible ventures thanks to a very particular

---

[130] *Pietas*, translated variously as "duty", "religiosity" or "religious behavior", "loyalty", "devotion", or "filial piety" (English "piety" derives from the Latin), was one of the chief virtues among the ancient Romans. It was the distinguishing virtue of the founding hero Aeneas, who is often given the adjectival epithet *pius* ("religious") throughout Virgil's epic *Aeneid*, where, unlike other heroes in other epic poems, Æneas feels compassion even for the defeated and for those he had to kill. The sacred nature of *pietas* was embodied by the divine personification Pietas, a goddess often pictured on Roman coins.

[131] *Hybris* (from ancient Greek: ὕβρις) describes a personality quality of extreme or foolish pride or dangerous overconfidence, often in combination with (or synonymous with) arrogance. In its ancient Greek context, it typically describes behavior that defies the norms of behavior or challenges the gods which, in turn, brings about the downfall of the perpetrator of hybris.

cocktail of *sensitivity*, even *vulnerability* (elsewhere in the opera – that is when, by a miracle and thanks to his proverbial skill in swimming,[132] he would succeed in escaping from shipwreck – he is not ashamed to confess that he is bewildered and afraid), great *flexibility* (here is *agility* again: mental and therefore vocal) which was transformed into *unpredictability* for his enemies; all crowned with a supreme *acumen* of intellect.

Here is the text of the monologue, as it came from the pen of that *Carneade* of genius whose name we shall now be obliged to remember: Nicola Francesco Haym.

Alma del gran Pompeo,	alma*ddelgəranəpoməpæo*
che al cenere suo d'intorno	kkealəcenerəsuodinətorəno*
invisibil t'aggiri,	inəvisibilətaggiri*
fur'ombre i tuoi trofei,	ffurombəre*ituœitərofæi
ombra la tua grandezza,	ombəra*llatuagərandezza*
e un'ombra sei:	eunombərasæi:
così termina al fine il fasto umano;	kkozittærminaləfine*ilfastoumano*
Jeri chi vivo occupò un mondo in guerra,	iæri*kkivvivokkupao*ummondoinə guærra*
oggi risolto in polve un'urna serra.	aoggi*rrisaolətoinəpolve*unurənasærra*
Tal di ciascuno, ahi lasso!	ttalədiciasəcuno*ahilasso
il principio è di terra,	iləpərincipioædditærra
e il fine è un sasso.	eiləfine*æunəsasso*
Misera vita!	mmizeravita*
oh, quanto è fral tuo stato!	oqquanətoæffəralətuosətato*
Ti forma un soffio,	ttiforəmaunəsoffio*
e ti distrugge un fiato.[133]	ettidistəruggeunəfiato*

---

[132] «Both Plutarch and Suetonius relate how in the harbor of Alexandria [Cæsar] escaped from the Egyptians by swimming some distance, almost a quarter of a mile, according to Suetonius, at the same time holding up "diverse books" to keep them dry. Plutarch adds that his enemies "made towards him with their oars on every side" and "shot marvelously at him" and Suetonius that he drew "his rich coate armour after him by the teeth, because the enemy should not have it as a spoyle."»; The Arden Shakespeare - University Press edition of W. Shakespeare's *Julius Caesar*, edition of 1973 (general editors: Prof. H. F. Brooks and Prof. H. Jenkins), note relating to verses 99 -144.

[133] "Soul of the great Pompey, who all invisibly surround his ashes, your trophies were shadows, your greatness a shadow, and you are a shadow: such is the end of human splendour; yesterday he was

Nameless buffoons

> *I can give neither name nor surname of that person, neither a title, not even a guess as to any of this [...] despite a lengthy search to make out his name, almost as if the pen might have caught fire [...] he who, thanks to the – let's call it blessed circumspection, not to give it a harsher name, of our writers – we shall be forced to refer to as the unmentionable.*
>
> Alessandro Manzoni,
> I Promessi Sposi

Verdi refuses to give a name to the Duke of Mantua[134]: it will never be given to us to know his name. When the assassin Sparafucile[135] asks Rigoletto "...*il nome?*" of the man he is to kill, the answer comes: "*Egli è delitto, Punizion son io.*"[136]

One's *given name*, in fact, is what seals up the secret of a man[137], the witness to his essence and humanity – a gift in which the Duke is completely lacking; let him, therefore, be satisfied with his noble title, only in virtue of which can he permit himself the kind of life he leads. Not only this, but the handsome young *anonymous* lover will, furthermore, give a false name (*Gualtier Maldé*) to the court jester's luckless, tender young daughter, who loves him: *Gilda* (from the Germanic root *gelb/gild*: "yellow, gold, shiny" – a name that immediately says everything about her worth and her purity[138]).

The girl takes her first steps in the mystery of love moving across the insidious ground of this fictitious name, warbling to us about it with all the tenderness and grace of a budding ballerina doing her first exercises at the bar and concluding her treacherous dream with a fatal promise: *fin l'ultimo*

---

alive, taking part in war in this world, today an urn encloses his ashes. Ah! woe is me! So are we all, we begin from earth, we end under a stone. Wretched life! Oh, how frail is your condition! A breath forms you, a breath destroys you."

[134] He was King Francis I in Victor Hugo's play *Le roi s'amuse* – upon which Piave based his *Rigoletto*, therefore Verdi's was a deliberate choice.

[135] Idem: the mercenary killer has a nickname, but no real name, unlike his sister: Maddalena.

[136] "He is Crime, I am Punishment".

[137] The Latin locution *nomen omen* means "a man's fate is in his name".

[138] In Hugo her name is simply *Blanche*.

sospir, caro nome, tuo sarà.[139] This promise will be fulfilled: after all, for so pure a soul, seeing the man to whom she has entirely devoted herself getting mixed up with another woman in a brothel, and all this shortly after hearing this same man swear eternal love to her, constitutes a sort of *deal-breaker* with life. It is necessary to restore order: the *sacred*, faced with *desecration*, is restored by *sacrifice*.

Gilda will go to her death dressed, significantly, in men's clothing, dying in order to save a man whom she has heard with her own ears declare that *la donna* (!) *è mobile*[140], while there he is, cuddling the first girl he comes across minutes after having been worried about his *angiol caro"*[141], after having thought himself truly in love and having decided to go and save her, when really he was merely very vexed by the offence that his pride had suffered, and thirsting for vengeance.[142] Alas, all it needed was for him to find a brothel on his way to save her and he was distracted, giving up his noble intention and furthermore saving his conscience by singing his famous song, in which he seems even to want to unload the responsibility for his inconstancy onto Gilda – inasmuch as she is *donna* and therefore *mobile*.

Instead, it is evident that the only *mobile* one in the opera is he himself – the *senzanome*[143] – and he is even just a little bit *donna*, if we look carefully: the fact that Sparafucile could imagine that he might pass off Gilda's body for his, even by means of the dramaturgical ploy of the sack, is suspicious: also taking into consideration the metaphysical and metaphorical sense of the story, we can only deduce that the Duke was more or less delicate and decisively more ephebic and feminine than virile and masculine.

This exchange of sexes, bodies and identities is highly significant. Gilda, the hero; Gilda, the "real man", whereas the Duke is the *female* and the *whore*: much more so than Maddalena, whose biblical name suggests her

---

[139] "Even my last breath, dear name, will be yours."

[140] "Woman is changeable."

[141] "Beloved angel."

[142] *Ella mi fu rapita! E chi l'ardiva? Ah, ma ne avrò vendetta! Lo chiede il pianto della mia diletta.* ("They have carried her off! And who dared to do this? Ah, but I'll have vengeance for it! The tears of my dear girl demand it.") - F.M. Piave, libretto of *Rigoletto*.

[143] "nameless one". In the Saragozza neighborhood in Bologna there is Via Senzanome, so called exactly because it was reserved for brothels.

redemption and whose pity for the Duke leads us to believe that it is certainly not the job that makes the prostitute. (Verdi furthermore had a lot of sympathy and a certain respect for authentic ladies of the oldest profession, whose humanity he praised – Traviata *docet.*) Also, Maddalena flirts with the Duke because *io l'amo, ei m'ama e perché è bello*[144]: because she likes him, in other words, and not for *work;* she even *cries* (just like the Maddalena in a bible picture) at the idea that Mantova might die assassinated. She appeared to be laughing at his courtship (*Ha ha! Rido ben di core ché tai baje costan poco)* [145], but in the end it will be the tears that she sheds at the idea of his ending up by being killed, that convince Gilda to sacrifice herself for him – *for them*.

The Duke sleeps like a log through all this because he, on the other hand – who would defy armies of husbands and lovers[146] merely to satisfy a whim, or so he says – does not care for anything or anybody (Maddalena calls him *signor l'indifferente;* just like any perfect pathological narcissist he does not suffer from the nuisance of feelings and, as for human passions or the love felt by normal people, he *derides* them (as Maddalena has it: *vi piace canzonar*).

The opera is all about the dichotomy of *riso* and *pianto* – laughter and crying; the Duke's narcissistic and unsentimental derision, incapable of human empathy, is moreover similar and identical in its effect – if differing in its cause – to the buffoon Rigoletto's *professional* variety: the two antagonists are united under the curse of *not being able to do anything except laugh;* even though for very different motives.

And just see, neither of the two grimacing buffoons has a Christian name: *Rigoletto* is, in fact, a nickname (in French *rigoler* means *to laugh*), not a given name. We shall never know the profound identity even of the hunchback, even admitted that he knows it himself, though his daughter begs him at least to reveal to her what his name is. Together with the name, Verdi takes away another important *retaggio d'ogn'uom* ("inheritance of man"), that is weeping: *il pianto*. When Rigoletto finally weeps, Verdi

---

[144] "I love him, he loves me and because he is handsome."

[145] "Ha ha! I'm having a good laugh, for such jokes cost but little."

[146] *Anco d'Argo i cent'occhi disfido, se mi punge una qualche beltà* ("I defy even the hundred eyes of the Argonauts if I fancy some girl or other").

underlines this epic moment of unmasking the truth with the monumental *parola scenica*: *Ebben, piango*.[147]

So the Duke is no more than a *beautified* hunchback, or Rigoletto an *uglified* Duke. Both anonymous and therefore impenetrable: it is understandable why a solitary and immured young girl like Gilda should have sought her own father figure in a young man who is not unlike Rigoletto, if not so from the exterior.

But, to come back to us: how can we portray in prosody, in words, in diction, the psychology of a disturbed young man who does not respect anything, who does not believe in anything, who laughs at everything and mocks it? Exactly as Verdi did, either in *Questa o quella* – an aria that is nothing more nor less than a (sublime) tavern song, in the most classical Italian tradition, with the typical ternary bass in *tonic-dominant-tonic* – as in *La donna è mobile* – which, on the other hand, is nothing more than a musical representation of a *fat laugh*, in which Verdi's typical *oom-pah-pah* in 3/8 time becomes a *Ha! Ha! Ha!* – the bursts of laughter beautifully matched to the doublings.

Our Busseto peasant has created, therefore, in this Duke's last aria, a *double parola scenica* –literary and rhythmical together.

Here we offer the text, with the diction on the right, of what is perhaps Verdi's most famous aria: a text that we are accustomed to hear badly deformed even when given by the voices of the most famous singers of the rôle, even though Verdi has written it razor-sharp. We now invite the reader to try reading the orthoepic version on the right and to enjoy every detail of the sounds.

La donna è mobile qual piuma al vento, muta d'accento e di pensier.	lladaɔnnaæmmaɔbilequaləpiumaaləvænto* mmutadaccæntoeddipenəsiæro*
Sempre un amabile, leggiadro viso, in pianto o in riso, è menzogner.	ssæmpreunamabile* lleggiadrovizo* inəpianətoinərizoæmmentzognæro*

---

[147] ("Well, then, I am weeping") Immediately afterwards Rigoletto turns to *Marullo*, because he is the more humane and, in fact, referred to by name, while Borsa only merits a nickname that tells us a lot about his greedy nature (*borsa* meaning "purse").

È sempre misero chi a lei s'affida, *chi le confida mal cauto il core!*	æssæmpremizerokiallæisaffida* kkillekonəfidaməlcautoiləcaore*
Pur mai non sentesi felice appieno *chi su quel seno non liba amor!*	ppurəmainonəsænətesifeliceappiæno* kkissuqquelsenononlibamore*
La donna è mobil...	lladaonnaæmmaobilə*...

Beats of twin souls

> *Non posso da te viver disgiunto,*
> *se non si smembra l'unità del punto.*[148]
>
> Gian Francesco Busenello,
> libretto of L'Incoronazione di Poppea

Monteverdi, in the concluding number of what would be the last operatic work in his brilliant career, and therefore in what was a kind of artistic and spiritual last testament, had to succeed in an impossible task: to get the audience to digest a finale in which the baddies triumph, disgustingly happy and happily together with impunity after having done their worst to everybody around.

Only the beauty of *Pur ti miro*, their love duet placed right at the fall of the curtain, could manage to gild so bitter a pill for the audience and make them applaud a fellow who, to put it euphemistically, could be described as hateful – remembered by history as a tyrant, a furious madman, whom, in the course of the opera, we see force his own old master to kill himself and who sends his wife into exile to die of hardship– together with the mistress whom he crowns queen.[149]

It almost seems to me that the divine Claudio does all this on purpose, as if he wanted to demonstrate to us – more than his uncontested genius – a new theorem, or at least show us a different reality, superior to the emotional,

---

[148] ("I cannot live separated from you, unless the unity of the point is split.")

[149] Nerone: "Law is for servants, and if I want to I can abolish the old and admit the new... [...] He who can do anything he wants is never in the wrong... [...] Hey there, one of you go quickly to Seneca and order him to die this very day!" - libretto of the opera, Act I.

commonplace one ruling the actions of the ordinary man; a *meta-moral* reality, that can be understood and resolved only in music.

It must be said, to start with, that this genius from Cremona was a lover of dissonances, to the extent that he was publicly scolded for this passion of his[150]. In various places in his works he exploits the phenomenon known in acoustic physics as *battimenti* ("beats"): because of which the *sinusoids* of two simultaneously produced sounds that are *extremely* close to each other in intonation (between major and minor seconds, into the smallest fractions of the tone), begin to physically *hammer at one another* – rather as if they were two little snakes in the mating phase – producing acoustically a characteristic *wah-wah* (similar to the effect of the electric guitar bearing this name).

A useful image for this embrace between evil people, that of two snakes who, in mating, get caught in each other's coils.

To scientifically demonstrate the *rightness* (little he cares for *justice*) of this love between the two *serpents*, Monteverdi resorts to the acoustic phenomenon of *beats*, applying it to the technique of composition, and in *Pur ti miro* succeeds in his attempt to *couple* the sound waves of the two singers' voices – both of them sopranos – making them sing so close to each other in pitch, as if they were almost one and the same voice, that in some places they become absolutely indistinguishable and alternate in singing identical phrases a major or minor second apart, exactly so as to obtain those *beats* that resemble the movements of a coupling.

Nero and Poppea are destined to love one another because they are – precisely – *on the same wavelength* and for this reason their love is *right*, in the sense of *exact*. This is the theorem that the otherworldly beauty of *Pur ti miro* demonstrates – infallibly. And from the point of view concerning this treatise, that of the word, there must necessarily be an embrace, complementary to the melodic one: and the librettist Busenello obtains it – ça va sans dire – through the *vowels*, managing skillfully to play upon the volumetric complementarity of the closed and open vowels, as if they were the *male* and the *female* of an electric wall socket, the key and the keyhole

---

[150] G.M. Artusi, *L'Artusi, overo Delle imperfettioni della moderna musica*, Venezia, Giacomo Vicenti, 1600.

of a lock, the clapper and the bell, the concave and the convex. In this way he came to create a tangible verbal *high relief*, giving one of them open and feminine vowels (*a, æ*) like coils in which the other sets about nestling acoustically with vowels that are closed, pungent, male (*i, e*); and then he inverts them, to demonstrate the *double-face* essence of the two lovers, their perfect identity, the fatality of their love, their being *soul mates* (although *black souls*, since we are discussing *Nero*[151]).

Here is the text of the duet, in the orthoepic version, beginning from the *adagio*:

(POPPEA / NERONE) *Pur ti miro / pur ti godo* *pur ti stringo / pur t'annodo* *più non peno / più non moro* *o mia vita / o mia vita* TOGETHER *o mio tesoro*	ppurətimiro / ppurətigæodo ppurətistəringo / ppurətannæodo ppiunnompeno / ppiunnommæoro ommiavita / ommiavita ommiotesæoro

Then, in the *presto* – which imitates the climax of a coupling, of every coupling – the librettist maintains the vocalic debate this time also by analogy, as well as by contrast, (see below): we have already mentioned the close relationship of the vowels *u* and *i*, but here he also plays about with the consonants: the *sighs* and *groans* are expressed by the *sibilants* and desire is expressed through the *dentals* – all of this in the context of the most typical wedding night phrases such as we might hear in a modern film – in a *crescendo* building up to the canonic *Sì! Sì! Sì!*. Then they begin again from the beginning, until at last, through a clash of intervals of seconds the two lovers come together on the note *G* and on the vowel *i*, the *dotted* vowel, as though they were, together, just one thing.

---

[151] From the Latin *Nero, -onis*; male proper name, III declension; *nero* in modern Italian meaning "black".

(POPPEA / NERONE)	
Io son tua / Tuo son io,	iosonətua / ttuosonio
Speme mia / Dillo, di'	spæmemia / ddilloddi
Dillo, di' / Tu sei pur	ddilloddi / ttussæipur
Speme mia / L'idol mio	spæmemia / llidoləmio
Dillo, di' / Tu sei pur	ddilloddi / ttussæipur
L'idol mio / Dillo, di'	llidoləmio / ddilloddi
Tu sei pur / L'idol mio	ttussæipur / llidolmio
Sì, mio ben / Sì, mio cor	ssimmiobæn / ssimmiocaor
TOGETHER	
Mia vita, sì sì sì!	mmiavitassississississi
Mia vita, sì.	mmiavitassi

Here the *unity of the point* is thus demonstrated: Monteverdi was clearly referring to a *note*, to a *unison*, furthermore on one vowel, and that vowel crowned by a *point* (i.e. a dot: *i*).

Formula for ruling the movement of the stars

CALAF (raising his arms to the sky):
Alba, vieni! Quest'incubo dissolvi!

Adami e Simoni, libretto of Turandot

We cannot digress here about the quality and quantity of symbolic and esoteric content in *Turandot*[152] and so we will examine – as was almost obligatory – the particular *aria* from it which is so famous that even whoever knows nothing about Opera knows it (probably thinking of it as a *song*, since it is often placed in anthologies of national classical *pops*, especially in the post-Pavarotti era): the *Nessun dorma*.

---

[152] We refer the reader to a marvelous interview with Roberto De Simone, on the occasion of his production of the opera at the Teatro Comunale, Bologna, in 2012 (available on the Opera House's YouTube channel).

Interpretative diction | 137

To begin with, *Nessun dorma* ("none shall sleep") is a command, the verbal tense employed being the exhortative subjunctive. The man singing orders the *popolo di Pechino* ("people of Pekin") to alter their natural bio-rhythm and stay up all night, in order to help find out the name of the Unknown Prince[153]. For this reason Calaf wants dawn to come soon, before anyone can discover what his name is: for his name is, in fact, the price that he has set on Turandot's freedom (he will, in the end, reveal it to her, so that she can freely choose her destiny[154]), after having solved her riddles and so acquired the right to marry her and through her *be made king*[155].

To achieve this, he orders the night to dissolve and the stars to set[156] by means of a *cosmic invocation*, so that the rising of the sun can bring victory (*all'alba vincerò*, "I'll triumph at dawn") of *good* over *evil* – the latter traditionally represented by *darkness*, by the shades of night.

The prodigy in question is really and truly an *exorcism*[157]; the case in point represents the liberation of Turandot from the hold of her ancestor Lou-Ling, who prevents her from loving and from uniting herself to the Masculine. This exorcism is to be effected through a *kiss*, for the kiss involves an exchange of *saliva*[158] which is crucial to the outcome[159], and by the Unknown *pronouncing his own name* on the lips of the *Principessa di Morte* ("Princess

---

[153] Of the symbolic significance of the concealed name we have already spoken, but here the audience gets to know, through Liù, that the Prince indeed has one, which Turandot does not know. LIU (watching the Prince with infinite tenderness, then turning to Turandot:) "I know his name… It is my wild delight to keep it secret and so I alone possess it!" - G. Adami, Libretto of *Turandot*.

[154] The faculty of choice, although sometimes dramatic and dilemmatic – leading even to self-extinction, preferable to subjugation – is a distinctive psychological trait of Puccini's extremely modern heroines, who are real women of our times, despite their archetypical aspects.

[155] This is the third and last riddle: *Gelo che ti dà foco e dal tuo foco più gelo prende! / Candida ed oscura! / Se libero ti vuol ti fa più servo. / Se per servo t'accetta, ti fa Re!* ("Ice that gives you fire and from your fire takes more ice! / Pure yet mysterious! / If she wants you free, she turns you into a slave. / If she accepts you as slave, she makes you King!"); libretto of the opera, Act II.

[156] «Then Joshua spoke to the Lord on the day when the Lord delivered the Amorites before the children of Israel; and he said in the sight of Israel: "Sun, stand still upon Gibeon; and you, Moon, in the valley of Ayalon."»; Joshua 10:12.

[157] The reader is referred once again to the interview with M° De Simone quoted in note 152.

[158] In many Biblical passages Christ frees from demonic possession or cures the sick by the application of his own saliva.

[159] We have seen in note 1 that Schneider brackets *canto-stone* with *canto-singing*; here we quote this association again, demonstrating that *incantesimo*, made up from *canto*, contains both concepts, *incantesimo* ("enchantment, spell") and *pietrificazione* ("turning to stone").

of Death") at dawn, that is *quando la luce splenderà* ("when light will shine"). This liberation will allow the cycle of life to continue, the sun to rise, the nightmare of the curse to end.

In order to perform any kind of magical or extraordinary event, as is well known, a *spell* is needed; a magic formula that, like chemical ones, must be absolutely precise in order to achieve the desired effect and not something much different, if not catastrophic (as we learn from the famous mishap of the *Sorcerer's Apprentice*).

It is not by accident that the English word *spell*, as a noun, means "incantation, charm, spell"[160], but also "lapse of time" in which something happens; while in its verbal form – *to spell* – it means "to indicate the spelling", "to go through the letters of a word, one by one, in the right order".

This is because certain words or letters, *chanted* in the correct order and in the right rhythm, work as spells, as charms, and produce mighty effects. On the other hand, if they are wrong or spoken at the wrong speed or in the wrong tone of voice, they can produce disastrous ones. But let us see how Puccini has set the words of this aria to music, in order to verify if it answers, in its intonation and diction, to the requisites of a magic formula, a *spell* that might result in a prodigious event of cosmic proportions, having the power to break a curse.

Speaking from the musical point of view, in this *aria* we are in the context of the key of G major. The Italian for "G major" is *Sol maggiore;* but in Italian *sol* is also "the sun", so that we find ourselves with the equation *G=sun;* the sun is precisely the star which is desired to rise with the prodigy. We find the aria beginning in the dominant of G major, though: it begins in D, which in Italian is *Re*: but, again, in Italian the word *Re* stands for both the note D and for "king", the sovereign whom the Prince is getting ready to become through the sacred royal wedding with Turandot. So the equations are now two: *G=sun, D=king*. Such an opening in D, anticipating the finale, is to be understood as *modal*: a kind of Gregorian *protus* (the first mode of the Gregorian system: especially since we are dealing with Puccini, a professional

---

[160] The formula *abracadabra*, apparently stemming from the Aramaic *Avrah Ka Dabra*, probably means "I create with the word/ as I speak".

organist and *maestro di cappella* since he was a teenager,[161] and his evoking of a far-off Orient). Calaf joins in with a propitiatory chanting, a sort of gregorian *anthiphon*, declaimed on a so-called *tenor*[162] and all articulated on the *finalis* [163] of the mode (the D): a *formula* that he repeats twice, an octave apart (*Nessun dorma... Nessun dorma*).

This *Re* ("D") must then find its way to its own *dominant*: the A. The A is, harmonically speaking, a *secondary dominant* to the main key of G, as well as the *repercussio* (a sort of dominant in the Gregorian modal system) of the *protus D* which, in fact, echoes itself and *rebounds* in the very heart of the spell (at the words *notte, tramontate*). Yearning for its *repercussio* A, the *finalis* D makes its way to it first through chromatisms and a succession of chords (with which Puccini masterfully depicts the transfiguration of night into dawn), but then, above all and distinctively, by means of a major scale of a fifth[164]: D-E-F#-G-A. This does not happen without first passing, for the glory of the tenor, through the high B *echappé*, which is the *major third* of the opening key of G major, which now becomes the fourth degree of the

---

[161] Puccini descended from a family of organ players – *maestri di cappella* at the Lucca cathedral for as many as four generations and, before that, musicians of the prestigious Cappella Palatina of the same city – and he himself started to play the organ in churches around Lucca "as soon as he was old enough to", which was when he was about fourteen years of age, to contribute to the family's finances; they had been left penniless when his father Michele, who was as well a respected teacher of composition at the local conservatory, passed away when Giacomo was only five years old. Giacomo later attended the same conservatory (the Istituto Pacini) as a student of a former pupil of his own father.

[162] See the voice "Gregorian chant" in the "Micro-history of vocal music" paragraph on page 33 of this book. Many of the greatest aria melodies by Puccini (although not only by him, naturally) are a kind of *tenor* psalmody; think of Johnson's *Ch'ella mi creda* in *La fanciulla del West*, and both of Cavaradossi's arias in *Tosca*, and even Tosca's *Vissi d'Arte*.

[163] In the Gregorian modal system, what we would now call the "tonic" of each mode was called *finalis* because the musical scales were thought of and performed from their highest note down, so that the tonic was the final note. This way of conceiving the scales was due to the fact that music was considered to be a gift of the Gods, coming from above.

[164] This very scale, in an analogous *magical* context, is not new to Opera, it represents a *formula of love* whose efficacy has already been tested: it is the same scale that, played in G (there's our G again!) – G,A,B,C,D – by Prince Tamino on the *magic flute* and by feathered Papageno on the *Glockenspiel*, acts as a shield against the forces of the Night (with its Queen in command), and as a lure for the friendly ones of the three boys, besides, naturally, his beloved. Once only will this scale be heard in *G minor*, when Papageno is on the very point of committing suicide, since he has lost all hope of ever finding his own true love, of joining himself to his mate and of procreating (the appearance of Papagena will follow at once!).

final tone of D, with which it forms a *plagal cadenza* IV-I that is absolutely typical of the Gregorian period and style.

The real *key* of the piece is finally unmasked: the *D major/Re,* the *King* status, conquered through the heroic climb up this musical and *existential* scale.

Let the *tenor* be careful, then, to clearly articulate this *spell* of the *Sol-Sun*, if he wants Turandot to make him *Re-King*:

Nessun dorma! Nessun dorma!	nnessunədaorma* nnessunədaorma
Tu pure, o Principessa,	ttuppureoppərinəcipessa
nella tua fredda stanza	nnellatuafəreddastanza*
guardi le stelle	gguarədilesətelle*
che tremano d'amore	cchettəræmanoddamore*
e di speranza…	eddisəperanza*
Ma il mio mistero è chiuso in me,	mmailəmiomisətæroækkhiuzoimme
il nome mio nessun saprà! No, No,	ilənomemionessunəsapra*nnaonnao*
sulla tua bocca lo dirò,	ssullatuabocca* llodirao*
quando la luce splenderà…	qquandollalucespəlendera
Ed il mio bacio scioglierà Il silenzio	edilənmiobacioschəoglierailəsilænəzio
che ti fa mia.	kkettifammia*
Dilegua, o notte!	ddilæguaonnaotte*
Tramontate, stelle!	ttəramonətatesətelle*
All'alba vincerò!	allaləbavinəcerao

Whirlwinds of joy

> VIOLETTA: *Da molto è che mi amate?"*
> ALFREDO: *Ah sì, da un anno.*[165]
>
> Francesco Maria Piave,
> libretto of La Traviata

Not for three days, nor for two months, nor from infancy; when Alfredo declares his love to Violetta, he has loved her – precisely – for *a year*. But why exactly *for a year?* And what dramaturgical necessity was there, that Verdi should make Violetta ask this question *onstage* and receive an answer so precise and yet so unconnected to the plot[166], within the economy of a libretto so absolutely condensed and devoted to action in every syllable, like every other Verdi libretto?

To look backwards a moment, in the prehistoric background of *La Traviata* we find – curiously – a *yearly* motif. It is February[167] 1852, Verdi is in Paris, but he has just received a commission from the Teatro La Fenice: they want a new opera to be staged a year later, at carnival time – as in the best Venice tradition. Without having the least idea of what subject to propose, all those available seeming weak to him, he happened to see a performance of *La Dame aux Camélias* by Alexandre Dumas *fils* and he fell for the heroine of the drama – the *demi-mondaine* Marguerite Gautier.

---

[165] "Have you loved me long?" -"Ah yes, for a year."

[166] The contrast with the clumsy affirmation of Baron Duphol just beforehand is, however, extremely significant, for it stresses that for someone in love a year is a whole lifetime, whereas for someone who is not in love it is less than nothing:

GASTONE (softly, to Violetta) Alfredo is always thinking about you. [....] You were ill, and he came here anxiously every day to ask how you were...

VIOLETTA (to Alfredo) I thank you. (to the Baron) You, Baron, did nothing of the kind...

BARON I have only known you a year.

VIOLETTA And he, only for a few minutes.

FLORA (quietly to the Baron) You would have done better to keep quiet.

[167] February, let us remember, will later in the opera be the month of Violetta's death, during the Parisian carnival, which we can hear "going mad" offstage.

La Traviata saw the light of day at the end of exactly a year of gestation on the part of the composer, during the carnival celebrations of 1853. Carnival fell late, that year, in the first days of March – the première was on the 6th, which, curiously, was the very date on which Dumas makes his Marguerite die in the novel, whereas the original Plessis (Alphonsine Rose Plessis, later ennobling herself into *Du Plessis*, lover of *Du-mas* as well as of various other noblemen of Paris, whose last names typically began with *Du-*) died, like Verdi's Violetta[168], in the first days of February, as we can read on the headstone of her grave in the cemetery of Montmartre, where she is buried near to the writer who has endowed her with immortal fame.

When the opera received its first performance, then, Verdi too, just like his Alfredo, had loved Violetta exactly for *a year*. A year was exactly the length of time that Verdi needed to unfold his most important and famous opera[169], beginning from the moment in which his heroine appeared before him; an anniversary he cleverly celebrated by interlocking one carnival with another: that is, transposing the death of Violetta, from the Parisian carnival of 1852, on to the Venetian carnival of March 1853.

The ancestral carnival tradition imposes the giving up of eating meat (and of all the pleasures of the flesh) as a start to the purification of Lent. In almost all cultures the carnival ritual foresees a *sacrifice*[170]; the killing of an equivalent of the *bue grasso*[171] ("fatted ox"; in Italy a puppet representing Carnival itself is often burnt) and it is celebrated with an exuberance that in some countries still actually bursts into orgies. It is followed by the forty days of Lent, which awaits the spring and Easter resurrection. Carnival would therefore seem the period of the year most appropriate for the immolation

---

[168] Note the constant lingering of the *flower* motif – symbol of sexuality and of the rebirth of spring – in the heroine's name: from Alphonsine *Rose* in real life, to Dumas's *Marguerite*, and Verdi's *Violetta*.

[169] According to a precise (and correct) answer given in the context of an Italian television quiz show (*L'Eredità*, introduced by Fabrizio Frizzi, an Autumn 2017 episode), on planet Earth *La Traviata* is performed at least once a day in some part of the world.

[170] "*Conosca il sacrifizio / Ch'io consumai d'amore / Che sarà suo fin l'ultimo / sospiro del mio cor*" ("Let him know the sacrifice/of love that I made/that I will always be his/until the last sigh of my heart); F.M. Piave, libretto of the opera, Act II.

[171] *Di Madride noi siam matadori / Siamo I prodi del circo de' tori / Testé giunti a godere del chiasso / Che a Parigi si fa pel bue grasso* ("We are the matadors from Madrid/We are the brave men of the bull-ring/ Just now come to enjoy the noise / that they make in Paris for the fatted ox"); F.M. Piave, libretto of the opera, Act II.

of a prostitute who has every intention of being born again by the purification of her ashes.

All this process of death and rebirth is repeated every year, *every blessed year*. For a year is a *circular* unit of measuring time, it is a *route* that starts from a beginning and that same beginning returns, after some developments and passing through a death. A year is, in fact, a complete *solar cycle*. A year is exactly the time occupied by a pirouetting *waltz*[172] round the sun on the part of the Earth.

The question that we have decided to ask ourselves in the context of this treatise is: is this *principle of circularity* reflected in the words of the libretto? What if the libretto were even based on this principle? Do we encounter this circular principle in its words, its adjectives, in its *parole sceniche?* Even the profane eye can see at once that *La traviata* opens and closes with the same word: *joy.*

It shines forth in Violetta's opening speech (*Flora, amici, la notte che resta d'altre **gioje** qui fate brillar*[173]), as well as her very last (*Ah, ma io ritorno a viver: oh **gioja**!*[174]). We are being stimulated into enquiring: but what is it, this *gioja*?

An excellent definition of the concept is offered by the American psychoanalyst Alexander Lowen, father of the Bioenergetic technique. In his essay entitled, exactly, *Joy. The Surrender to the Body and to Life*[175], Lowen writes: «*Joy is a religious experience. In religion it is associated with surrender to God and the acceptance of his grace.*» In the light of "Addio del passato" (*A lei, deh, perdona, tu accogli, oh Dio!*[176], we can only confirm that in Violetta this surrender is effectively accomplished. Lowen then goes on to make a crucial linguistic observation: «*The Hebrew word for joy is "gool". Its primary meaning is "to spin around under the influence of a violent emotion".*

---

[172] There are many waltz rhythms (a circular dance if ever there was one) in the opera in question: the most famous is the *Brindisi* ("drinking song") in Act I.

[173] "Flora, friends, make what is left of the evening radiant with joy"

[174] "Ah, but I'm coming back to living again: what joy!"

[175] Alexander Lowen, *Joy - The Surrender to the Body and to Life*, Penguin Arkana, 1995.

[176] "Ah, grant her forgiveness, Oh God!"

This word, which the Psalmist used to describe God, pictures him as whirling with sublime delight.»

In Italian the word *gioia* is derived from the Latin *gaudia* (plural of *gaudium*): note how the root "*gaud*" (from whence also come the verb *godere*, from *gaudere*, through crasis of the "au") pronounced in the American manner becomes indistinguishable from *God*. Since *gioia* and *gaudio* are, in all their declensions and variants, more than synonyms: they are exactly the same thing.

Similarly, *gioco* ("game") and *giogo* ("yoke") are also derived from this same *gioia*. There is one *gioco* in particular that consists exactly of the same mechanism as the yoke, applying the concept of *whirling joy* described by Lowen: it is the one so marvelously referred to in English as the *merry-go-round* and that in Italian is called *giostra* or *carosello* (from *garosello*, diminutive of "*gara*", therefore "little duel"), since it derives from medieval *giostre* ("tournaments"). These *giostre*, if played between whole teams and not just by single knights, were called *tornei* [177] (*tournées*, from the French *tourner*, 'to turn round": for they were seasonal, like the modern *champions league*) and they were fought entirely on horseback (thus explaining the presence of horses on today's roundabouts for children).

Having made these linguistic comments with Lowen's help, let us pass on directly to list here below some well-known passages from the libretto. The examples in the text would be too numerous to list here, especially if we mentioned all the variants and synonyms of the concept of *gioia* included therein (*felice, lieta, diletto, piacere, riso, giuliva*, etc.), but here follows a select list, which also includes some phrases that have passed into common everyday usage:

- ✓ **Giocammo** da Flora... e **giocando**...[178]
- ✓ Flora, amici, la notte che resta, d'altre **gioje**...[179]

---

[177] On this medieval and chevalresque note we could open an entire chapter regarding the close thematic relationship between *Trovatore* and *Traviata*, but we shall abstain, postponing the treatment of this question to another place.

[178] "We were gambling at Flora's ... and playing..." (Chorus, Act I).

[179] "Friends, for what remains of the night, other joys..." (Violetta, Act I).

- ✓ Sì, la vita s'addoppia al **gioir**! [180]
- ✓ Tra voi saprò divider il tempo mio **giocondo**...[181]
- ✓ **Godiamo**, la tazza e il cantico...[182]
- ✓ **Godiam**, fugace e rapido è il gaudio dell'amore... È un fior che nasce e muore [183] né più si può **goder**, ah! [184]
- ✓ Si **ri-desta** in ciel l'aurora e n'è forza **ri-partir**... Nel **ri-poso** ancor la lena si **ri-tempri** per **goder**... Mercè a voi gentil signora di sì splendido **gioir**! [185]
- ✓ Oh **gioja** ch'io non conobbi...**gioir**! Gioir! Sempre libera degg'io folleggiare di **gioja** in **gioja**... **Nasca** il giorno, il giorno **muoia**...[186]
- ✓ Qui presso a lei io **ri-nascer** mi sento, e dal soffio d'amor **ri-generato** scordo ne' **gaudi** suoi tutto il passato.[187]
- ✓ Tu **r-ammenta** pur nel duol ch'ivi **gioja** a te brillò ...Al tuo vecchio genitor...tal **gioja** non negar.[188]
- ✓ "Più tardi la **ri-vincita**" ... "Al **gioco** che vorrete"[189]
- ✓ Le **gioje** e i dolori tra poco avran fine...[190]

---

[180] "Yes, life is doubled when you enjoy yourself!" (Chorus, Act I).

[181] "I'll be able to share my times of joy with you all" (Violetta, Act I).

[182] "Let's enjoy the glass and the song" (All, Act I).

[183] «Another view of joy is given in Schiller's poem *Ode to Joy*, in which joy is described as fashioned from celestial flame with the power to entice the blossom from the bud, draw sun from the sky and "set spheres through boundless ether spinning". These images suggest that God in heaven can be identified with those cosmic forces which create the stars, the most important one for life on Earth is our Sun. It is the celestial flame, the spinning sphere whose rays make the earth fertile, [...] setting in motion the dance of life.»; Alexander Lowen, *Op.Cit.*

[184] "Let's enjoy ourselves, the joy of love is fleeting... It is a flower that is born and dies and one cannot enjoy it any more, ah! " (Brindisi, Act I).

[185] "Dawn wakes in the heavens and we must go away... In sleep we'll get back our strength for enjoyment!" (Chorus, Act I). Not by chance, the libretto is full of verbs composed with the prefix *ri-*, to underline the endemic cyclicity to which the opera is subject.

[186] "Oh joy that I never knew before! Joy! Joy! Ever free I must skip madly from joy to joy... whether the day be dawning or dying..." (Violetta, finale Act I).

[187] "Here, near to her, I feel reborn, and in the breath of regenerated love I forget the past in the joys she brings" (Alfredo, Act II).

[188] "Remember in your sorrow that there joy shone on you.. Do not deny such a joy to your old father" (Germont, Act II).

[189] "Revenge comes later on" – "I'm ready to oblige you" (Barone and Alfredo, Act II).

[190] "Joys and sorrows will soon be over" (Violetta, Act III).

- ✓ *Prevenirvi volli una **gioja** improvvisa!* [191]
- ✓ ***Gioja** improvvisa non entra mai senza turbarlo in mesto core...* [192]
- ✓ *...la tua salute **ri-fiorirà**!* [193]
- ✓ *Amato Alfredo! Oh **gioj**a! ...in me **ri-nasce**... m'agita insolito vigore! Ah, ma io **ri-torno** a vivere! Oh **gioja**!* [194]

In this new light, the central theme of the opera seems to be clearly outlined: when all is said and done, it does not have very much to do with the superficial and rather banal plot about the persecuted great love of a provincial (or *Provençal,* as it may be) boy for a tart, who almost as a punishment dies of consumption: rather a scanty plot for managing to make this opera into what it has become, unequalled in history, thanks to Verdi's work (without which Alexandre Dumas *fils* would have remained less than the shadow of his own *vecchio genitor* ("old father"), who was no less a celebrity than the author of the *Count of Montecristo* and the *Three Musketeers*).

La Traviata seems to be decidedly sprung from and animated by a *lògos*: the immortalizing, whirlwind principle of *joy* of which Lowen speaks, which reconnects with the Eternal whoever surrenders to its grace, spinning round, whirling *di voluttà ne' vortici* ("in the whirlpools of pleasure"). Before fulfilling her ultimate sacrifice of joy, Violetta clearly specifies that she is "returning to live again" and there you are: this final *palingenesis* of hers is, in our view, the demonstration of the theorem of the existence of the *linguistic archetype* which is the elixir of immortality both of the heroine and of the opera itself; perhaps it is the elixir of immortality of Opera *tout court*, as a *genre*, risen to be a new mythology of the newly founded Italian nation. To quote Fellini again, in the marvelous extract reprinted at the beginning of this book, he opens his mythological and mythopoeic vocation of Opera for Italy with the phrase: *"These things are so much ours that they become extraneous, like the subconscious."*

---

[191] "I wanted to prepare you for an unexpected joy!" (Annina, Act III).

[192] "Unexpected joy never enters the sad heart without upsetting it" (Violetta, Act III).

[193] "Your health will bloom again!" (Duet, Act III).

[194] "My beloved Alfredo! What joy!... In me I feel new stirrings of life... Ah, but I'm coming back to live again! Oh joy!" (Violetta, Act III).

In the DNA of *La Traviata*, reposing in the *national collective subconscious* of Italy, there really is written the *gool*, the *gioja vorticosa* ("spinning joy"), that, with incredible intuition, Fellini describes in a quotation with which we opened this treatise and that now returns – *circularly* – to close it: «...*suddenly everything coagulates, as if it were all drawn together by some eternal law that makes you spin round marvelously [...] Perhaps that particular opera, La Traviata, is absolute perfection, a sphere*».

The essence of *Traviata*, then, is permeated by that same cosmic whirl that animates the motion of the planets and the cycle of the seasons, the *spin* of electrons and everything that spins eternally, impelled by the unstoppable force of an intrinsic regulatory plan. Just as in Dante's astronomy it is *Amor che move 'l sole e l'altre stelle* ("Love that moves the sun and the other stars"), so also for Verdi and Piave *Amor è palpito dell'Universo intero* ("Love is the *pulsation* of the entire universe"). In any case, *a-mor* (*alpha privative* preceding the Latin *mora, -ae*: "pause") means no more than without *end*, without *death*. *Amore* e *Morte* was, in fact, the original, oxymoronic title given to the libretto by Piave, but perhaps it would have been inappropriate, seeing that death in its sense of a definite stop is a concept quite extraneous to this opera, which is a waltz of life, death and inevitable *rebirth*.

It seems tremendously to the point, and almost predestined, that the opera should have been commissioned by the Gran Teatro La Fenice: this name was chosen for the building because of its tormented history of disasters – numerous fires and reconstructions have followed its fortunes until our own day. The name was inspired, as a good-luck charm, by that mythological bird capable of regenerating herself cyclicly after having died from self-combustion. Verdi donated his own *phoenix* to the Teatro La Fenice, at the same time endowing the mythological Olympus of the forthcoming Italian nation with what would be her most immortal goddess of joy.

Conclusions

We opened this book by relating how, in the Florence of 1600, the *Camerata de' Bardi* engaged in creating Opera modeled on Greek tragedy, borrowing its myths, and now we close our book having established and demonstrated how this Italian adaptation of classical culture ended up by creating a new national Olympus, which, exactly like the Greek one, studs the calendar and celebrates its annual liturgies with new rites, mixing up these new pagan deities of a vocal nature with Christian saints and martyrs. The temple of Demeter and the cult of her daughter Persephone have given place to the temples of Opera where Mimì – whose real name we know to be *Lucia*[195], meaning *light* – meets Rodolfo every freezing Christmas night[196] to ask him to light her *candle*, symbolizing the sun triumphantly reborn[197] at the winter solstice; thus her putative "mother", Violetta, is immolated as a sacrificial victim at Carnival only to be reborn, an immortal phoenix, with the arrival of Easter; neither can *l'april*[198] flower again if Calaf does not melt the ice and the enigmas of Turandot, and fails to chant the spell of his own name upon her lips at the birth of every new day.

---

[195] «Mi chiamano Mimì, ma il mio nome è Lucia [...] Mi chiamano Mimì, il perché non so...», "They call me Mimì, but my name is Lucia [...] They call me Mimì, but I know not why..."; Giacosa and Illica, libretto of Puccini's *La Bohème*, Quadro I. The nickname *Mimì* might be an onomatopoeic rendering of the chirping of the swallow, a bird to which she is compared by Rodolfo (*Torna al nido, la rondine, e cinguetta* – "The swallow goes back chirping to her nest").

[196] Saint Lucy is celebrated in Italy on the 13th December; the 7th December is, on the other hand, Saint Ambrose's day. Sant'Ambrogio is the patron saint of Milan, and on his day, by tradition dating back to 1940, La Scala opens its annual Opera season (for the previous 140 years it had been inaugurated on the 26th December).

[197] The Enciclopedia Treccani declares: "[Christmas] is believed to be of Roman origin and it is certain that towards the middle of the 4th century it was celebrated on the 25th December. This choice influenced the Roman civil calendar which, from the end of the 3rd century, celebrated the winter solstice and the birth of the "victorious sun" on that day; this is why Christians wanted to oppose the pagan holiday and superimpose on it the festival of the birth of the true sun, Christ."

[198] «Là sui monti dell'Est la cicogna cantò. / Ma l'april non rifiorì, ma la neve non sgelò. / Dal deserto al mar non odi tu mille voci sospirar:/ "Principessa, scendi a me! / Tutto fiorirà, tutto splenderà!" Ah!», (" Over there, on the Eastern mountains, the stork was singing / But spring did not flower again, but the snow did not melt/ From the desert to the sea, do you not hear a thousand voices sighing: / "Princess, come down to me! / Everything will bloom, everything will shine"); Giuseppe Adami, Libretto of *Turandot*, Act I.

In this manual we have touched upon some essential points with the intention of opening some matters, but not of closing them; of encouraging interrogatives, more than furnishing definitive answers; all the rest must be taken on rôle by rôle, aria by aria, syllable by syllable, vowel by vowel, with your own coach: now we know that each word, if wisely pronounced, is a *spell*, that might set off a *motion* of cosmic import.

Whoever deluded himself, when getting hold of this book, that because of it he would be able to do without a maestro truly expert in the *materia prima* of Opera will have understood, reading it, that it was written in order to spread exactly the opposite message: no singer, in no phase of his studies or his career, can ever do without such a person. A person who, in the best of all possible worlds, would coincide with that of the singing teacher; and when the latter might seem inadequate, the former may constitute an excellent compensation for him, and he will always be the ideal complement even of the best voice teacher. For a singer enjoying a career, moreover, a similar resource will end by being an insurance for the success of each single performance, even when this has to be undertaken in conditions of temporary vocal indisposition.

Besides singers, however, we warmly recommend in particular the reading of this text to accompanists and *répétiteurs*. The Italian ones working abroad find themselves often, and against their will, burdened with the job of *Italian diction coach* in the Opera houses for which they work, without having the least idea of what they themselves are doing when they speak (even supposing that they speak correctly) or where to start from in teaching such a kaleidoscopic subject, connected with *every* aspect of operatic performance. Choir masters and orchestral conductors will find it a precious instrument for understanding the score and the potentialities of a libretto; and they will know, after reading it, how best to guide the singers entrusted to them. Composers, for their part, will have more background knowledge in setting to music verses or simple phonemes. Finally, as far as *stage directors* are concerned, it cannot too often be repeated that **the staging of an opera begins from the interpretation of the text,** which, as we have seen, is literary *and* musical at one and the same time, and gives birth to the score: without stage direction of the *musical text*, an opera is no more than a stage setting. (Between ourselves: the English and the French direct better than the Italians, because the Italian language by reason of its nature does not need stage direction, being *in itself* theatrical, malleable, visible and scenic: Dante wrote a *Comedy* that does not need stage representation because it was to the Theatre what Bach's *Art of Fugue* is to Music: we are talking about *absolutes* that are enough unto themselves, created for pure contemplation.)

It goes without saying that an Opera *coach* in language and diction cannot be any individual whatsoever who happens to be of Italian nationality (neither need he be so, so long as he is *really* properly prepared). A degree in literature serves but little; one needs specific skills, *technical-vocal*, *musical* and *dramaturgical*, to do this job as it should be done. We hope, therefore, that the Conservatories will hurry to provide their pupils with teachers trained in these specific skills and *create* specific diploma courses in this discipline as soon as possible, to properly equip those who will go out in the future to teach and promulgate it.

We hope that we have validated, in what we have written, the biblical text according to which the power of the *word* is of cosmogonical importance.

It can not be, nor must it ever more be, in the light of this text of ours, that people neglect the power of the *enchantments* that are produced by this language that has generated – among the other parallels, of varied nature, as we have seen – that universe imbued with the genius of Italy that for four hundred years we have called Opera.

Appendix: Exercises

How to work

1. **In the column on the left, copy *by hand* the original Italian text** of the piece you want to study (we will here repeat our example: *Voi, che sapete*).

2. **In the column on the right, create its orthoepic version**, according to all the prescriptions of this manual. That is:

   a. **underline the only tonic vowel of every word** (if not sure about which one it is, check where the accent of the word falls in a dictionary);

   b. **mark every tonic open *e* / *o* as æ / ɶ** (check the orthoepy of every tonic *e* and *o* in a dictionary to make sure whether they are open or closed);

   c. **add all syntactic germinations** (mandatory doublings);

   d. **insert the *schwa*** where necessary or opportune;

   e. **keep visually together all that is to be sung in one breath**;

   f. **notate the breaths** with the sign "*", or another of your choice.

Original	Orthoepic
Voi, che sapete	vvo̲ikkessape̲te
Che cosa è amor,	kkekkaɶza æamo̲r*
Donne, vedete	ddɶnnevvede̲te
S'io l'ho nel cor.	ssio̲laɶnnelǝcaɶr*
Quello ch'io provo	qque̲llokiopraɶvo
Vi ridirò;	viridiraɶ*
È per me nuovo,	æpperǝmennuaɶvo*
Capir nol so.	kkapi̲rǝnnolǝsaɶ*
Sento un affetto	ssæ̲ntounaffæ̲tto
Pien di desir	piæ̲nǝdidezi̲r*

Ch'ora è diletto, *Ch'ora è martir.* *Gelo e poi sento* *L'alma avvampar,* *E in un momento* *Torno a gelar.* *Ricerco un bene* *Fuori di me,* *Non so chi 'l tiene,* *Non so cos'è.* *Sospiro e gemo* *Senza voler;* *Palpito e tremo* *Senza saper,* *Non trovo pace* *Notte né dì:* *Ma pur mi piace* *Languir così...*	kkoraæddilætto* kkoraæmmarətir* ggæloeppɔisænto laləmavvampar* einummomento tornoaggelar* rricercoumbæne ffuɔridime* nnonəsɔkkiltiæne* nnonəsɔkkosæ ssospiroeggæmo* ssæntsavoler* ppalpitoettræmo* ssæntsasaper* nnonətrɔvopace nnɔtteneddi* mmappurəmipiace llanəguirəcozi...

3. Translate the original Italian text into your mother tongue, using the left column for a literal translation, and the right column to add subtexts and psychological nuances, that will come in help in the process of interiorization of the text, both mnemonic and interpretative.

Literal Translation	Subtext
You, who know *What love is* *Ladies, see* *If I have it in my heart*	You, who know love better than I do For you are women, (and therefore gentle spirits, and lovely, and also older, and therefore wiser)

	See and tell me if what I am feeling (for you) is real love (because I must find a way to confess to you that I love you, Countess)
What I am feeling *I will tell you* *It's all new to me* *I can't understand it*	I will try to explain what I feel, Something I have never felt for anybody else before, So with the excuse of not understanding it, I will tell you about it, And I am going to make a declaration of love to you,
	Hoping to seduce you with my singing, Because I know you love to sing too, and sing well, and like music as I do (my love)
I have a feeling *Full of desire* *Sometimes it's joy* *Sometimes it's suffering*	I have feel a feeling of love that is full of desire, and it can be Heaven or Hell,
I freeze and then I feel *My soul burst into flame* *And the next minute* *I'm freezing again… etc.*	and makes my blood pulse with passion and the fear of losing you… etc.

The student should now proceed to practice on pieces from the repertoire of his own choice, according to the rules and advice offered in this manual.

In the remaining pages of this book he will find exercises expressly designed and space specifically structured for his study.

Here the Author takes leave of her reader, wishing him *buon lavoro.*

1. **In the column on the left, copy *by hand* the original Italian text** of the piece you want to study.

2. **In the column on the right, create its orthoepic version**, according to all the prescriptions of this manual. That is:

   a. **underline the only tonic vowel of every word** (if not sure about which one it is, check where the accent of the word falls in a dictionary);

   b. **mark every tonic open *e* / *o* as *æ* / *ɶ*** (check the orthoepy of every tonic *e* and *o* in a dictionary to make sure whether they are open or closed);

   c. **add all syntactic germinations** (mandatory doublings);

   d. **insert the *schwa*** where necessary or opportune;

   e. **keep visually together all that is to be sung in one breath**;

   f. **notate the breaths** with the sign "*", or another of your choice.

3. **Translate the original Italian text into your mother tongue**, using the left column for a literal translation, and the right column to add subtexts and psychological nuances, that will come in help in the process of interiorization of the text, both mnemonic and interpretative.

1. **In the column on the left, copy *by hand* the original Italian text** of the piece you want to study.

2. **In the column on the right, create its orthoepic version**, according to all the prescriptions of this manual. That is:

   a. **underline the only tonic vowel of every word** (if not sure about which one it is, check where the accent of the word falls in a dictionary);

   b. **mark every tonic open *e* / *o* as æ / ɶ** (check the orthoepy of every tonic *e* and *o* in a dictionary to make sure whether they are open or closed);

   c. **add all syntactic germinations** (mandatory doublings);

   d. **insert the *schwa* where necessary or opportune;**

   e. **keep visually together all that is to be sung in one breath;**

   f. **notate the breaths** with the sign "*", or another of your choice.

3. Translate the original Italian text into your mother tongue, using the left column for a literal translation, and the right column to add subtexts and psychological nuances, that will come in help in the process of interiorization of the text, both mnemonic and interpretative.

1. **In the column on the left, copy *by hand* the original Italian text** of the piece you want to study.

2. **In the column on the right, create its orthoepic version**, according to all the prescriptions of this manual. That is:

   a. **underline the only tonic vowel of every word** (if not sure about which one it is, check where the accent of the word falls in a dictionary);

   b. **mark every tonic open *e* / *o* as *æ* / *ɶ*** (check the orthoepy of every tonic *e* and *o* in a dictionary to make sure whether they are open or closed);

   c. **add all syntactic germinations** (mandatory doublings);

   d. **insert the *schwa*** where necessary or opportune;

   e. **keep visually together all that is to be sung in one breath**;

   f. **notate the breaths** with the sign "*", or another of your choice.

3. **Translate the original Italian text into your mother tongue,** using the left column for a literal translation, and the right column to add subtexts and psychological nuances, that will come in help in the process of interiorization of the text, both mnemonic and interpretative.

Appendix: Exercises | 167

1. **In the column on the left, copy *by hand* the original Italian text** of the piece you want to study.

2. **In the column on the right, create its orthoepic version**, according to all the prescriptions of this manual. That is:

   a. **underline the only tonic vowel of every word** (if not sure about which one it is, check where the accent of the word falls in a dictionary);

   b. **mark every tonic open *e* / *o* as æ / ɶ** (check the orthoepy of every tonic *e* and *o* in a dictionary to make sure whether they are open or closed);

   c. **add all syntactic germinations** (mandatory doublings);

   d. **insert the *schwa*** where necessary or opportune:

   e. **keep visually together all that is to be sung in one breath**;

   f. **notate the breaths** with the sign "*", or another of your choice.

3. Translate the original Italian text into your mother tongue, using the left column for a literal translation, and the right column to add subtexts and psychological nuances, that will come in help in the process of interiorization of the text, both mnemonic and interpretative.

The Author

Sara Gamarro (Mola di Bari, 1981) is an Italian soprano and an internationally renowned coach for the diction and interpretation of Italian Opera.

Apulian born, raised and currently based, she studied composition and took her diploma in singing, receiving her education mainly from the Bologna Conservatory, and then specialized in Opera stage directing at the Scuola dell'Opera Italiana of the Teatro Comunale in the same city.

She has prepared her most illustrious pupils for their débuts in the world's leading Opera houses under such conductors as Lorin Maazel, Simon Rattle, Antonio Pappano, Fabio Luisi, Giancarlo Andretta, James Levine, Tito Ceccherini, Yannick Nezet-Seguin – among others.

She teaches at the Accademia del Belcanto of the Festival della Valle d'Itria in Martina Franca (IT) and she is also Italian Libretto Instructor for the Göteborgs Operan (SE), and Opera North (UK).

Following her intense activity in teaching and spreading the Italian operatic culture on line, in 2018 she founded Stato dell'Opera, the first web Opera company to come into existence.

Cantare Italiano is her first book.

The Translator

Michael Aspinall (Stockport, 1933) was educated at the Manchester Grammar School and Manchester University, graduating in Italian Language and Literature.

He studied singing in London with Antony Benskin and in Rome with Vincenzo D'Alessandro and Adolfo Baruti. Aspinall made his début as *The Surprising Soprano* in Rome in 1969 and has presented his operatic parodies with his own company in Italy, France, Spain, Switzerland, the U.S.A., Great Britain, Germany, Denmark, South Africa and Australia. In Italy he has been the guest of, among others, the Teatro La Fenice, Teatro San Carlo, Maggio Musicale Fiorentino, Accademia Filarmonica Romana, etc.

He has written sleeve notes on historical singers for EMI records, Nimbus, Romophone and Marston Records. He writes regularly for the magazines Musica (Varese, IT) and The Record Collector (London). As a research consultant in Italy he has worked with the London Opera Society, Opera Rara, and with many singers, including Montserrat Caballé. For nearly thirty years he has been the official English translator for the Rossini Opera Festival of Pesaro.

From 1997 to 2009 he taught singing at the Conservatorio of Trapani (Sicily). From 1997 to 2004 he taught every summer at the Belcanto Festival of Dordrecht, Holland, where he also directed several operas.

As a co-author he published a biography of Enrico Caruso (Longanesi, Milano 1990) and *Gioachino Rossini, compositore, cantante e bon viveur* (Conservatorio Nicola Sala, Benevento, 2010). He edited a new edition of Nicola Vaccaj's *Metodo Pratico di Canto Italiano per Camera* (Edizioni Zedde, Turin 2000).

Global Print S.r.l. Gorgonzola (Mi) - marzo 2022